CHILDREN COME FIRST
The Inspired Work of English Primary Schools

CASEY and
LIZA MURROW

American Heritage Press   New York

For Bobs and Dick
Janet and Ed

Contents

Introduction

THROUGHOUT THE 1969–70 school year, we were fortunate observers of English primary classrooms. In schools concerned with the whole life of the child, we found an approach to learning vastly different from education as we know it in many American public schools. In these remarkable classrooms, children come to know themselves—and each other—more fully. They are involved in learning that is deeply important to them, encouraged by innovative teachers whose positive attitudes toward children are reflected in each child's successes. The children who attend these schools find both constructive guidance and a setting that is adaptable to their needs and concerns.

It is clear to Americans who have visited these schools that many aspects of primary education in England could be applied with great success in the United States. The opportunity to look across the Atlantic for ideas and advice adds another dimension to the debate about elementary education in America. It also offers alternatives for those parents, teachers, and administrators in the United States who are aware of the need for radical change in the schools.

Despite nationwide concern about the appalling emotional and physical conditions of some American classrooms, little has been done to improve them on any wide scale. Statements like the following, written in 1969 by John, a twelve-year-old friend of ours in Washington, D.C., are still too common:

> . . . my teacher was talking to us so I asked what was we going to do today and she said "You be quiet" so I was quiet until I saw her giving us some old work so I asked "Why do we do the same work day after day?" She must of got mad and she hit me with a ruler twice, once in the face and once on the arm. I got so mad that I walked out of the room to go and cool off.

John's brave expression of his feelings, which probably reflected the silent thoughts of his classmates, brought the immediate pain of the ruler and, later, the difficulties of a day's suspension over the incident. When we talked to John afterward, we realized that underlying his confrontation with the teacher were many more unspoken and deeply serious questions about the quality of his life in school.

If John and his teacher had known one another, he might also have asked: What does this work and my experience in school have to do with my personality or my own interests and abilities? Do you really believe in what you are teaching me or do you, too, obey higher and meaningless commands? How can I make sense out of the long, wasted hours I spend here?

Unfortunately, John's case is not unique. It has been described in different ways by John Holt, Herbert Kohl, Jonathan Kozol, Nat Hentoff, and others. Americans who are aware of the plight of John and the thousands like him know that many American public schools today do not respond to the needs and concerns of individual children, black or white, rich or poor.

As teachers, we have undertaken this study of a system other than our own because we are concerned about the state of education in America. During the school year 1969–1970, we visited forty primary schools in England to gain an understanding of the ways in which children learn in a variety of settings. We devoted the greatest portion of time to classroom observation, visiting some schools for a day, others for longer periods. We gained substantial information from interviews with head teachers—the men or women appointed to run the school, with duties comparable to those of an American principal—and classroom teachers in every school we visited. Our inquiries took us also to colleges of education, where teachers are trained. We talked with people involved in many aspects of education, from teachers in small village-schools to administrators in the central government.

During these visits, we were impressed with a variety of achievements on the part of individuals and of whole schools. The schools we saw were not experimental. We visited outstanding schools in areas of deteriorating housing, in impoverished coal-mining towns, in rural villages, and in wealthy suburban communities. The excellence of these schools does not result from a massive influx of money or an attempt to concentrate talent, creating distinct "model" schools as we have seen in the United States.

Although some attitudes and patterns of living differ in England and America, the similarities are great enough to allow Americans to draw examples from the work of English schools. Certainly, these schools are beset by many social problems that are familiar to Americans. Oversize classes of forty or more are common, and funds, despite government efforts at aid, are insufficient to enable rundown urban areas to cope with their difficulties. Personal insecurities, cramped living spaces, and broken homes, frequently found in industrialized nations, combat the best efforts of teachers and schools in both countries.

In their upbringing and behavior in school, many English children are comparable to their American peers. However, there are important social differences. The class system in England is still a part of society and of education. In the eyes of many Englishmen, publicly operated schools remain an institution for the workers. Early upbringing is often more harsh in England than in the United States, and English children may come to school more docile than Americans. In affluent communities in England, children often appear more subdued in school than do their counterparts in the United States. When considering the work of these schools, we cannot ignore the danger of applying the successes of one culture to the problems of another.

While undertaking this study, we learned of a number of American misconceptions about English primary schools. These range from the idea that there is a single, dominant method of teaching in English classrooms to the more unfortunate assumption that moving the furniture implies a complete transformation of the learning experience. Americans have wrongly observed that in England the teacher plays little or no part in directing the child's learning. Some educators in the United States use the term "Leicestershire Plan" to describe the work of English primary schools.[1] This term has no validity. There are many different areas in England that can claim success in primary education.

Finally, there is an increased tendency on the part of some American visitors to England to speak as though all British primary schools had achieved a degree of excellence in education which is unknown in America. This misapprehension does little justice to attempts to improve the quality of education in the United States and ignores the reality of many British primary schools.

The attitude in many English schools, from those in transition to the most enlightened, is one of positive belief in continuing change. Few thoughtful British teachers would agree with this recently published optimistic statement made by an Australian professor: ". . . it could be said that the revolution in English primary education is now achieved."[2] On the contrary, recent estimates indicate that one-quarter to one-third of primary school children attend schools which provide them with a good, forward-looking education.[3] While this is a remarkably large group, the fact remains that the majority of English children are not fortunate enough to attend schools that fall into this category. In addition, enlightened education rarely extends beyond the primary level, and in many areas it is limited to the first three years of schooling.

Until recently, secondary schools were largely selective, with the best students going to grammar schools, which prepared them for universities. The rest of the children attended secondary modern schools of varying quality and were offered little chance of education beyond the age of fifteen or sixteen. Decision as to a child's secondary school placement was made largely on the basis of the "eleven-plus" exam, which was taken at the age of eleven and often sealed the child's fate. The secondary schools are still bound by traditional ideas; while most areas have abandoned the exam, the schools themselves are only beginning to change. This means that few children attending publicly supported schools have an encouraging or purposeful experience for their entire school careers. That fact hangs over some of the best work taking place in the early years.

The innovative approaches to learning that we describe in the first five chapters have taken many years to develop. They began in a few schools in the late 1920's and early 1930's. The ideas tested by small groups of teachers and researchers grew slowly because they demanded not only different techniques, but new attitudes on the part of many teachers. Changes originated in the "infant schools," which work with five- to seven-year-olds.[4]

The pioneers often worked on their own, with little support. Their ideas were in the liberal tradition of educators such as Pestalozzi, Froebel, and Montessori, but they were often unaware of these influences. It was not until the publication of the government's Hadow Report on education, in 1931 and 1933, that the work of these innovators was given any official recognition. The report praised what was taking place in some schools and urged more teachers to follow suit. While official support was thus given to education that treated children individually, it was not until after the Second World War that the ideas encouraged by Hadow became more widespread. The war had a tremendous effect on primary schools throughout England. Children were forced to move from the cities to the safer rural areas. With village schools overcrowded and everything in short supply, improvisation was essential. Infant-school teachers who were working at the time cite the war's influence on their teaching as far greater than that of any theoretician.

After the war, the opening of new schools aided change. The relatively small size of these schools, even in many cities, allowed for consideration of children's individual problems in a very natural manner. Head teachers and classroom teachers have been able to know most of the children in the building.

Since the 1950's, variations on traditional, formal teaching have gradually come to a few "junior schools," which work with seven- to eleven-year-olds. The abandonment of the eleven-plus exam by some local education authorities has allowed the junior schools to concentrate less on rigorous preparation for secondary school and more on the child as an individual with immediate needs.[5]

The most important development of the 1960's was the publication of a government report on primary schools. Officially titled *Children and Their Primary Schools,* this two-volume collection of research was published in 1967 and is commonly referred to as the Plowden Report after its chairman, Lady Plowden. It gave official sanction to progressive, informal classroom methods. Beyond this, it called for more attention to the breadth of a child's development and to the factors that affect his learning, both in and out of school. The Plowden Report has received much attention and has served as both guide and support for innovative methods in many schools.

A host of influences have contributed to the success of many primary schools in England. However, these schools do not yet represent a majority. Successful schools demand great commitment on the part of all concerned. A number of primary schools in England provide an education no different from that available forty years ago. Others have changed only teaching practices, but not ideals or goals. All of us can learn a great deal, however, from the achievements of schools where the child's experience has been deeply altered. Most of the schools we describe in the following chapters fall within the group that leads the country in change and innovation.

CHAPTER ONE

Days with Infants

SIX-YEAR-OLD DAVID runs up the walk, flings a farewell glance at his mother and the baby, and disappears toward his school. He is pleased with himself, the first one there. His friends will soon follow. With his entry into the building, the day can begin; the school comes to life.

The visitor who arrives at a British school before its official nine o'clock opening finds an atmosphere that differs radically from that of many United States schools at the same time of day. Standing on the grass, mothers talk with teachers or chat with friends. Children discuss things that have happened since the close of school yesterday; they hold hands, take a quick run around the playground, or swing on the parallel bars. No lines are formed outside the school, and it is very rare to hear a bell.

The noises are busy: a door opens and closes; the children talk as they go into school to take up unfinished work from the day before. Some go straight to the library corner and may read or look at pictures. Others search for friends and teachers in nearby rooms. In one class, a guinea pig escapes and is pursued from the paint corner to the cupboard under the sink, where the children try to coax it out with a piece of lettuce. There is much laughter and some singing. A child calls to a friend next door, "Come quick, our guinea's got out!" Some young volunteers arrive on the scene and plot a trap for their pet.

In the hallway, children move about purposefully or stand in small groups. A few boys gather around David, who has brought a caterpillar to school in a jar. His teacher comes through the door and approaches the group. "What have you got, David?"

"A caterpillar. I'm going to make him a cage."

"Get on with it, then!"

Four girls help their teacher, a young woman with a warm smile, to set up an exhibit of pottery just inside the front door. They are matching the browns and grays of the pots with bits of cloth dyed last week by their class. "Look, Valerie," says the teacher, "Here's what your Mum finished in pottery class last night." Valerie smiles, takes the bowl carefully, and holds it up for the others to see ("Ooh, that's lovely"). She finds a place for it on the table and agrees to work with her friend Helen on a sign that will explain the exhibit. They run off to their class to get started.

The door of the staff room opens, revealing a group of teachers waking up over a cup of coffee. The head teacher tells a story, and there is laughter and a general stirring as they leave each other for their classrooms. The head teacher stops in the hall to greet a parent. "Mrs. Barnes, you must come in and see the decorations in the hall." They go off together, but stop to allow Mrs. Barnes to experiment with a xylophone left outside a classroom. She picks out a tune and then smiles at the head teacher. They continue down the corridor.

The beginning of the morning in infant schools sets the tone for the day. The visitor can sense an open and relaxed atmosphere that makes these schools remarkable places for everyone involved. In the first minutes spent in such a school, it is evident that the major concern is the development of relationships between child and child, teacher and child, and teacher and teacher. The sounds of children talking, working, and singing throughout the building are themselves indications of the vibrant life of the school. The morning is soon under way.

In Bristol, a class of five-, six-, and seven-year olds is gathered in the hall of an old building.[1] A record player in one corner lets loose a rhythmical West Indian calypso, and the teacher, lost in the middle of her group of children, begins to dance. The children follow her and branch out on their own. Their bodies completely free, they interpret the happiness of the music with their arms, legs, torsos, and heads, and change their movements with shifts in the music. They are relaxed, aware of one another on the floor.

"That's lovely, Ian, lovely," says the teacher, her face flushed from the exercise. She stops the record, and the children gather around her or flop down on the floor. "Watch what Ian is doing," she says. The children make a space for the boy and watch as he moves to the calypso. As he dances, his face is open and smiling, yet intent on what he is doing.

Anyone who had seen Ian earlier that morning might have been amazed. He started off to school angry, having had little breakfast. Coal smoke sifted across rooftops and down into the street. A pale fog drifted across the chimneys. He crossed the remains of a river that carried garbage, old shoes, and sewage as it twisted past back yards filled with gray laundry. On the other side of the water his school sat waiting: a squat nineteenth-century building surrounded by an iron fence, its only playground a strip of asphalt at the rear.

Ian is West Indian, as are the majority of his classmates. His school has many characteristics of an impoverished school in a black neighborhood in the United States. Yet what goes on inside the building does not reflect the attitude of society which is evident in the building's rundown condition. When Ian came to school, he was not shouted at, or asked to line up, or expected to sit quietly through much of the morning. He was greeted by the head of the school, who gave him a hug, asked him how he was feeling, and said, "Hope you have a good day, Ian." Now he is deeply involved in the music, in the praise of his teacher, and in the expression of his feelings through movement.

As the record ends, the class moves across the hall. Small hands grip the waist of the child in front, and the snaking line follows the teacher into the classroom.

The teacher pauses at the door to take a little girl by the hand. Throughout the movement class this six-year-old child had been "hiding," secure in the fortress of an old sofa turned to the wall in a corner of the large hall. For some of the time she had been joined by a younger boy from another class. They had played a game that involved recognizing words on cards and then counting the cards to find the winner. Neither wanted to join his classmates. Instead, they sought out the soft cushions, the peace and privacy of the sofa. Teachers walked by and smiled at the pair, but never disturbed their sanctuary.

In a nearby classroom a small boy interrupts a story the teacher is reading to the class. Crouched on the floor, his head in his hands, Stephen breaks into a storm of tears. A sturdy boy slides over to him, touches his shoulder gently, and says to the teacher, "What's the matter with Stephen?" The teacher takes the small, crumpled Stephen into her lap. The older boy and the teacher learn that Stephen, still weak from a long illness, has bumped his head. Together they comfort him. The older boy pulls Stephen down beside him and the sobbing lessens and then stops as the teacher continues to read.

In Ian's classroom almost everyone has settled down to one task or another; they are relaxed and quiet after their dance—except Ian. Sometimes hostile and seldom able to concentrate for more than five minutes, he appears to be disturbing three or four others. He has refused two requests to come and read privately to his teacher. Knowing him well, she does not issue an order, but asks patiently.

A few moments later, Ian is ready to read—he demands to read—but the teacher is occupied with another child. He takes a friend (a better reader) by the hand and asks if he may read to him. They go into a corner and Ian begins. Another child comes near them, looking for something, and bumps into a chair and then into Ian's friend. Ian frowns at him and says, "Now if you weren't here that wouldn't happen, would it?" He starts to read again as the intruder departs quietly to return to his own work.

Ian dealt with this disturbance easily and without uproar because he was engaged in work he wanted to pursue. He had the help and support of a friend. He had no time for the disruptive response he would surely have made if he had been working on an assignment prescribed by the teacher.

Ian's infant school is in the port city of Bristol on the west coast of England. The slum area served by the school has yet to be recognized by the central government as eligible for additional Educational Priority Area money, although it meets the general standards. [2] The teachers, however, do not assume that all is lost or hopeless. They firmly believe that many of the children have something special to offer; that their needs are different from those of children in other parts of the country, and that the school must respond to them individually. The children do not conform to standards set by some distant, abstract authority. Instead, the school adapts to the lives of its children.

In the same city there is a very different school located in a rather ordinary, middle-class area where row upon row of identical houses stand behind well-kept gardens. The head of this school expresses much the same philosophy with an entirely different group of children. In this school as well as in the one just described, the character of the children and the staff is evident throughout the building. As the children work at reading, writing, building, dressing up, or painting, one can watch the life of the school revolve around their interests.

In a classroom at one end of the corridor, children read aloud to each other and to the teacher. A child explains his painting to a girl who looks on over his shoulder. Nearby, a child asks a teacher's aide how to spell "angel." Two boys stand at a picture window, observing birds outside through a pair of binoculars. A third boy identifies the birds in a book and adds their names to a record he is keeping. Four or five children work out some mathematical problems using colored tiles, while others write stories, using words that are as vibrant and alive as the conversations around them. As in many infant schools, there are forty children in this class. Though the teacher certainly feels the group is too large, she has made the best of it. While many different projects are under way throughout the room, the group is unified by a sense of purpose and well-being.

In the midst of all this activity a boy picks out a tune on a xylophone in the corner, and suddenly, spontaneously, the class breaks into song. The teacher stops listening to a child read. She smiles and adds a bit of harmony while the boy at the instrument continues to play. Next to him a friend holds two paper cups at their bases and brings the open ends together in a strong, staccato rhythm that keeps the beat for the class. As the music dies away, work goes on as before, without a pause.

These two infant schools seem to be very different at first glance. Certainly, the children who attend them come from dissimilar backgrounds. The first school gives a great deal of attention to the immediate physical and emotional demands of the children. The second school appears more intent on encouraging the children to bring their emotions and thoughts into the open. Yet, in many ways, the children are similar.

The head of the second school believes that all normal children are equal in two important ways: first, their ability to move and use their bodies and, second, their capacity to communicate through speech. These are the natural resources that teachers must utilize and develop to the fullest extent, realizing that they are qualities that will enhance the child's learning. The entire school reflects this philosophy. The language of the children is the basic tool through which they come to read. The learning of mathematics, their use of poetry, music, drama, and art, all closely relate to the movement and character of individual children.

This philosophy is a dynamic ingredient in many good infant classrooms. As in Ian's school, children throughout England are encouraged to talk to one another while they work; they move around the room and the school freely. A teacher who believes that children learn through conversation with others and through deep involvement—whether physical, emotional, or intellectual—with the materials at hand will not be excessively occupied with maintaining "order," "silence," or "control."

Noise is a matter of concern only when there is too much of it for people to communicate easily or when it disturbs children working alone. Order is achieved because the children are totally immersed in their work.

The teacher in a good English school is primarily concerned with the full development of each child. She hopes to introduce him to experiences which will help him to think clearly and imaginatively, to discover the pleasure of learning, and to understand himself and others more fully. She encourages a creative approach to problem solving and opens his eyes to the world beyond the school. Above all, the child's personality is of prime importance. Because he takes an active role in learning—and in doing so, establishes a firm relationship with the teacher—issues of order and control are seldom spoken of in good infant classrooms.

While individual schools and classrooms are naturally very different, varying according to the interests of the people working within them, there are many similarities to be seen in a number of infant schools across England. Classrooms do not mark the boundaries of the child's experience in school. The curriculum is seldom compartmentalized into reading, writing, arithmetic, and other disciplines. One of the most subtle and important aspects of these classes is the way in which barriers between disciplines have come down, allowing the children to be involved in a broader view of learning.

First and foremost the schools and the classrooms belong to the children.

The appearance and arrangement of classrooms in

many infant schools indicate how they are oriented to the children's needs. There are no desks in rows, no overwhelming blackboard toward which all eyes can be directed. Instead, there are these common features: small tables and chairs in groups; a sandbox on four legs, which can be moved outside in nice weather; a large, portable basin for water play; and a corner where painting and other messy activities take place. There is also a library corner. There is usually a counter or table covered with mathematics materials: objects for counting (buttons, shells, pebbles, tiles, pine cones), cards with math ideas on them, a small balancing scale. Much of the wall space is beautifully decorated with the children's work: paintings, poems, stories, descriptions of projects, puppets, collages—all representative of the children's interests. The room also reflects the talents of the teacher and contains, in corners and on tables, stimulative items and articles of interest that she has brought in.

In many classrooms the children make the curtains for the windows. They dye old sheets a solid color and then paint flowers and animals on the cloth. Or they may tie strings around bunches of the sheet and dip them in other dyes to create startling patterns through the process of tie dying. Thus, much of the classroom seems to vibrate with the things the children have made, as well as with the sounds and sights of work in progress.

The visitor familiar with American classrooms immediately notices that the teacher's desk is either nonexistent or pushed into a corner where it serves as another place to store papers, children's work, plants, and materials. When the children have a great deal of choice and freedom to move, the teacher's role is extremely dynamic. As she moves from one group to another, she engages in a variety of direct encounters with the children. She listens to three children read, starts others off on potato printing, observes a group working with numbers before talking with them about their work. She is constantly involved in eliciting responses from the children that tell her how much they understand about the material and how she can help them. Most of her work is extremely purposeful and structured.

The ways in which children learn in these circumstances are as varied as the children themselves. In order to talk about the process in greater detail, we must look at the arrangement of a child's day. It contains, within the changing activities and movements of the children, a very dynamic inner structure, established by the teacher and maintained by the children.

The morning usually begins with a meeting of the whole class. The children gather on the floor around the teacher and talk about what they want to do first. From past experience in the room and the school, they know the limits on their actions and, more important, the range of possible activities open to them.

Teacher and child know that some activities have specific places in the timetable. A period for physical education and perhaps a time for music are set aside. In addition, there are often tasks that the children must complete by lunch or by the close of school—drawing a picture and writing a story to accompany it, reading to the teacher or to a group, or working on a mathematics problem. This tacit understanding is essential to the successful operation of the classroom.

No teacher can keep track of up to forty children at every instant. In a classroom where children are seated passively and silently at their desks, the teacher can never tell what the children are thinking. In such situations—still the ideal for many English and American teachers eager to feel absolute control—it is impossible to ascertain whether the children are involved. They are asked to participate with only one sense at a time. They listen (or do they?); they answer a question (or try to). They watch as the blackboard is being filled and emptied, covered and erased. The whole child is rarely involved.

On the other hand, an infant-school teacher in many good English schools can glance around the room and discern whether her group is actively engaged in work. If not, there may be no need to scold—perhaps a child who appears idle is tired, in need of help, or lost in an important daydream. She trusts the children to take much of the initiative in their learning and she can watch them use every part of themselves as they do it.

Every class has its own manner of beginning. The early morning gathering provides a few moments for the teacher to be close to the children and for the children to be close to each other. Bodies touch; eyes and ears show eagerness to see and hear friends. Some children tell stories, while others listen to the teacher describe an evening spent with their parents or explain material they may use for a collage. It does not matter how the child communicates his plans, for the teacher usually understands him. He may say "I'll write," or "I'll be at the writing table," or just hold up his book and say "about the moon"—an idea he has for a picture. In any case, the teacher can see that he knows exactly where he is going, and a nod of her head and a smile of encouragement sends him on his way.

One by one, the children leave the group and spread out in the classroom. In these first moments, the teacher sees the individual rhythms of each child. Some are full of energy and need to move freely. Others want to sit down and work quietly. Because the structure

that holds the day together is complex and sometimes difficult to discern amid all the activity, we will
follow two infant-school children through a day to give
a clearer picture of what takes place.

Ann

Ann is a five-year-old in her second term at an infant
school in a suburban area. She is in a class of five-, six-,
and seven-year-olds and is engaged in a number of
activities which are leading her toward reading. Since
she did not attend a nursery, her first term in school
also involved a great deal of learning about how to get
along with the other children in her class.

On her arrival in school in the morning, Ann's first
concern is with some seeds she planted the day before.
She finds her name on a flower pot and looks carefully
into the dirt for signs of growth. She pokes the soil
gently with one finger. Satisfied that nothing has
happened, she joins the group seated on the floor and
asks the teacher if she may do a painting. The teacher
nods. Ann jumps up, puts on her smock, and goes to
the corner of the room where a large easel and paints
have already been set up. She fills the paper with vivid,
colorful strokes and lines, stopping now and then to
rinse her brush in the sink or to check on a friend's picture nearby. When the painting is done, her teacher
comes over to talk about it.

"What a lovely painting. Can you tell me about it?"

"It's a pattern that the sun makes."

They talk for a few more minutes. An older child
looks on and points out the painting to a friend. The
teacher gets a pencil. Ann asks her to write on the picture, "My sun pattern. By Ann," and watches carefully
as the teacher writes the bold letters beneath the
painting.

"Let it dry a bit," says her teacher, "and then come to me. We'll see if you're ready to trace over the words with a crayon."

A crate of milk has arrived. Ann takes her picture off the easel, hangs it over the drying rack, and takes a small container of milk to a table where one of her friends is sitting. They talk about the pet hamster that belongs to the class and take a look at him. Ann fills his water jar and runs her finger down his back. "So soft, his fur." She goes back to check on her painting. She takes it to a table, where the teacher helps her to trace over the letters. A boy looks over her shoulder and reads "My sun pat—." "Pattern," says Ann. The teacher tells the class to leave what they are doing and go out to play. When Ann returns, she finds that her teacher has mounted the painting on the wall.

Ann joins a friend at the water table—a large, movable basin on legs. Using a funnel, they pour water from large containers into smaller ones. Their teacher looks on and talks with them about which container holds more. Ann spends the rest of the morning with her hands and arms deep in the water. She and her friend talk vividly about the water, what it feels like, and whether it will spill as they pour. Ann is totally absorbed in the activity and surprised when the teacher's voice rises above the others in the room.

"Time to clean up. When you have put things away, come and sit by me." The children protest: "But we're not finished yet!"

"Don't worry," says the teacher. "You can go on with it this afternoon." Ann and her friend find a rag and mop near the tub of water. In other parts of the room, math cards are put back in boxes. Paintings are hung over racks to dry. All is accomplished within minutes, with few directions from the teacher. She trusts her class to do this, and she may well continue working with a child on some writing completed that morning or help only the youngest children in the class to clean up. As the children come to sit round her once again, a girl whispers in her teacher's ear.

"Mary wants to read her story to the class," says the teacher. Ann and her classmates listen attentively while Mary reads a tale of adventure. A group of boys announce that they want to display their work. They have made a dragon, a prince, and a princess out of tissue paper, tinfoil, and bits of cloth to illustrate a poem the class likes. The figures are paraded in front of the group while the teacher and the class speak the words of the poem. Small bodies sway back and forth to the rhythm of the poetry.

When the poem is over, Ann washes for lunch and puts on her coat. She is one of the children in her class who go home for lunch. Her mother waits outside, near the classroom door. "Come in and see my painting," says Ann. They look at it together and then leave the school.

By the time Ann returns from lunch, everyone else has come in from the playground. Some of the children are already at work. Ann asks her teacher what she can do. "Would you like to join Sarah in the Wendy House? You haven't played there for a few days." Ann enters the little door and dresses herself in a long skirt, high heels, and a cloak. With the two other girls in the house, she agrees that she will be the "auntie," while they play "mum" and "granny." They troop out the door of the Wendy House, pushing a pram, parade through the classroom, and go to the playground, where they continue to act. When they come back in, a short while later, they do not go to the classroom, but search out the head teacher, who spends some time talking with them about their play.

After a few minutes, Ann returns to her classroom, where everyone is changing for physical education. She strips to pants and undershirt and joins the others in the hall.[3] When the movement class ends, Ann spends the rest of the afternoon with Sheila, a seven-year-old from her class. They collect the eggs from the chicken coop owned by the school. Sheila asks Ann to count them and then checks her answers. Ann watches as Sheila records the number on a chart, which is kept in the corridor so that all can see it. Children in other classes sometimes make graphs based on the information on the chart. The two girls rejoin their class for a story read by the teacher. As the children leave, Ann checks on her seeds—still no sign of growth—talks briefly with her teacher, and joins her mother at the front door.

NIGEL

Nigel lives on the top floor of a ten-story building in a rundown section of London. He arrives at school bursting with energy, and has trouble sitting still when the class gathers around the teacher. "Can I take the blocks and go outside?" he asks. His teacher agrees and opens the door, helping him to carry the wooden blocks out to the paved playground. Until the break at ten thirty, Nigel spends his time building a large roadway. He comes back inside once to find some toy cars to run on the road. His finished structure extends a third of the way across the playground and includes complexes of bridges and intersections as well as the necessary garage.

At ten thirty his teacher, who could see him from inside the classroom, joins him outside. "What a marvelous job you've done, Nigel. And isn't it long—will you measure it after the break and find out how long it is? Ask a friend to help you. But now tell me about it; what's this?" Nigel walks from one end to the other, talking, describing, pointing.

After the break, Nigel and Peter use a yardstick and discover that the roadway is twenty-six-feet long. The teacher encourages him to draw a picture of the roadway and write what he discovered, pleased that from all she could see the boys had measured with great care. Nigel works quietly at a table, bent over a large sheet of paper. His time outside allowed him to work off steam, as well as to begin a project that he could happily carry on indoors.

At about eleven thirty, Nigel's teacher calls him over to join a small group seated around a table. Together they spend a few minutes working with math cards. Nigel shows his picture to the teacher. "After lunch I'm going to write about it," he says.

Rushing into the classroom in the afternoon, Nigel loses little time finding his picture book in his drawer. He writes, "I made a long road. Peter and I measured it. It was 26 feet." He takes the picture and the writing over to his teacher, reads what he has written, and talks with her a bit about it. When he leaves her, he joins a friend and they devote the rest of the afternoon until story time to fighting a severe "fire" that breaks out in the Wendy House. Fortunately, the classroom has two firemen's helmets and a few small fire-engine toys, which helps this game along.

While Nigel and Ann attend two very different schools, both their teachers believe firmly in the children's ability to make a number of decisions about the way they spend their time. This does not mean that the teachers avoid planning. On the contrary, classrooms that appear totally free are really skillfully engineered.

They must be if they are to succeed. The teacher needs to be clear about what each child has accomplished and what sort of work he needs to become involved in during the coming days. She must watch him carefully, noticing the kinds of play in which he engages and the development of manual skills. She records what he has accomplished. Nigel's teacher knew that on this day he had done some writing, worked on two kinds of math, and done a great deal of building. On the following day, she may encourage him to devote more time to reading.

The atmosphere at the end of a day in a good English infant school implies a great deal about the life in the classrooms. As children gather around teachers to listen to a story, they show few of the tensions that one can see in children who have passed the school hours in a regimented classroom where tasks are assigned and work begins and ends at arbitrary intervals established by the teacher.

As they pull on their coats to go home, a number of six- and seven-year-olds may carry a book from the school library. Whether they read it or not is up to them. There is never any homework in an English infant school. Homework as we know it almost always consists of written work meant to reinforce a skill acquired in school. Infant-school teachers prefer to develop these skills in the classroom, where there is access to help of all sorts and less risk that a child will complete work mechanically without understanding it. The work the children do in school changes from moment to moment. Their levels of achievement naturally vary so that no two children go home in the afternoon needing the same sort of work.

Infant-school children often find a day in school exciting. Each day brings new discoveries; a child may show progress in reading or develop the insight that allows him to move on to more difficult math. There is none of the unnatural competition of a traditional classroom; there are no grades and no tests. The competition that does exist—between the two children playing a card game in their sofa hideout, or in a group racing to see who can most quickly represent the "four table" using small tiles—is induced by the children, and those who compete do so by their own choice.

There is little pressure of the sort remembered by the parents of today's infant-school child. If a child reads slowly or with difficulty, he has the time to work on it without pressure. If he cannot manage math on a given day, his teacher is likely to accept this fact and think of how she may be able to help him get around his difficulty tomorrow. In either of these situations, the child often receives help from a friend and does not approach the teacher for aid every time it is needed.

Flexibility is the most important single feature of a day in a good infant school. If something unusual crops up, it often enters naturally into the class activities. When a head teacher in one school was given some intriguing pieces of glass, she brought them into a class and the children became involved with the shape, color, and feel of different pieces. A number of children spent the morning talking with the teacher about them, classifying the glass in different ways and experimenting with refraction in different kinds of light. No one required that these six- and seven-year-olds sort the objects in any way. No one defined refraction or even mentioned the word. What the children accomplished was the result of their own curiosity and the interest and encouragement of their teacher.

The flexibility of the day and the lack of a rigid curriculum allow the teacher to reorganize a few days or a week around a special goal if it seems needed. One teacher we observed in Yorkshire was concerned that her class of predominantly five-year-olds grasp the concept of a number and its value. She knew that many of her children could count from one to ten, but they had little understanding of the meaning of the numbers. As one solution to this difficulty, she organized each of ten days around a number. On the fourth day, for instance, she asked the children to group themselves in fours for short periods of time. They sang four songs before lunch, counted out the milk bottles in fours, and drew four pictures on a sheet of paper. When we visited the class, the children were clear that the number 4 accurately described four beans, four chairs, or four days. They had also come to grasp more abstract groups of four, such as asking four questions.

Although there are certain patterns common to infant-school classes, the variety of formats used by English teachers in planning their days is vast. No two classes, even in the same school, are exactly alike because the teacher's skills and the children's interests are drawn upon to structure the day and the work that takes place.

CHAPTER TWO

Spools, Cubes, and Conkers

WHAT GOES ON in the unusually good primary school is in many ways an extension of learning that began in the child's home and continues there. The attitudes are much the same. The teacher tries to respond positively to a child's needs, encourage him individually, give him a wide choice as to how he will learn, and establish a flexible timetable against which to measure him.

"What mother," asked a teacher in England, "would say to her child, 'Simon, you are now ready to walk,' and then force him to do so? Of course, she will help him when he tries to stand on his own. She will encourage him, but she can't tell him exactly how to do it, or determine the moment when the child is physically capable of launching out on his own. It's the same in the classroom. We are not going to force a child to read if he is not ready to. We help him with many tasks that are related to reading and we wait until he is ready to take the first mental step which is, for him, like the first physical step away from his mother's hands."

When the English child of five leaves home and goes

off to school, he is not entering a strange or bizarre world that has nothing to do with his first four and a half years. In a great number of cases, he enters a school that carries on the work of those important years in his family and gives him the added advantage of working and playing with children his own age.

George Dennison, in *The Lives of Children,* makes a plea for taking the work of the home and the nature of the child into account in American schools, just as many English infant schools have done:

> We do need to remind ourselves . . . that the gay intelligence of childhood is not the product of schools, but of family life and nature and certain of the accumulated experiences of our culture. It is what we *give* to the schools when we give them our children. If we were completely at a loss to state the positive goals of education, we might still insist upon a minimal responsibility: do not destroy what already exists.[1]

Dennison has a profound knowledge of what the goals of education should be. The description in his book of the First Street School is proof that teachers can accept children as they are and help each child to become more himself as he learns and grows. Teachers are working in a similar vein in a number of English primary school classrooms.

The way that teachers use materials in some areas of England is indicative of the manner in which many of them approach learning. Most English teachers are cautious about new systems or units prepared by curriculum developers. Few such programs exist in England. More common are publications which aid the teacher in working with the children in a certain field, typified by the work of the Nuffield Foundation in mathematics. The booklets published by the Mathematics Project are the product of cooperation between a foundation and a remarkable council, financed and supported by the government, local education authorities, and teachers.[2] Their booklets outline potentials for modern math in primary schools, but do not seek to dictate any one way of teaching. Full of informative material and examples of children's work, the booklets suggest approaches, possible projects, and essential concepts, but leave much of what might be called the mathematics curriculum up to the skill and the imagination of the teacher. One reason that teachers reject many more standard units is that these are usually restricted to limited subject matter, which calls upon the child to handle prepared material to the exclusion of his own interests.

Teachers in England also face a financial problem. The budgets of English primary schools are not large enough to outfit classrooms with expensive systems and kits. Although school budgets differ, the disparity seen in America between wealthy suburban districts and poor urban centers does not exist to the same degree in England. Teachers accept limited budgets and make many of their own materials.

Lack of money is never an asset, but it can provoke ingenious use of existing material. Junk often possesses greater potential for stimulating creative work than anything that is manufactured for specific classroom use. We have seen cardboard cereal-boxes and cartons of all shapes and sizes take on diverse and imaginative forms: a fire engine big enough to hold three volunteers; human-size robots; and a complete miniature carnival equipped with a Punch-and-Judy Show, merry-go-round, booths, and a ferris wheel. None of these projects was suggested by the teachers, who brought in some of the material and left the rest up to the children. Wood scraps, old machines, radios and clocks, bits of metal and wire are all transformed by the children and frequently provoke more learning than appears to be gained from a manufactured toy or gadget. Of course, for this sort of work to progress successfully, the staff must concur that a portion of a classroom can legitimately function as a workshop area, accessible to at least a small group of children at a time.

It bears repeating that work in infant schools is seldom divided into different disciplines—the traditional subjects. Hence the term "integrated day" is used by some teachers to describe the varied ways their classrooms work. Teachers bring as many disciplines to bear in every situation as they can, but they neither think or talk always in terms of these divisions of knowledge. The use of multicolored spools in an Oxfordshire school is indicative of an interdisciplinary approach to versatile materials.

In one corner of the classroom is a box of wooden spools, collected largely from sewing baskets in children's homes. Painted by the children, they are put to use in many ways. The youngest in the class build towers and cone-shaped structures, first using haphazard patterns, later distinguishing and grouping the colors, or making towers of uniform color.

A length of string turns the spools into beads, which can again be classified and ordered in a marvelous variety of ways. In this process, the teacher is not there to say "Now make me a string with just reds and greens," but rather to ask questions. "Can you make one with a pattern to the colors?" or "Will you make a string with your favorite color in the middle?" Each question calls for a distinct ability on the part of the child to classify and to repeat a pattern, but does not imply failure if he decides he cannot do it—or does not choose to.

This is far from the end of the spools' usefulness. A

balancing scale makes them useful for weighing and counting in relation to any other available objects. A well-supplied classroom will contain many items for comparison: marbles, dried peas, horse chestnuts, pebbles, and blocks of wood of various sizes.

The work with the spools calls upon the child's imagination and creative ability. He will probably be able to produce more combinations of colors than his teacher would think to suggest. Some important and difficult mathematical ideas are involved in the child's work. If, as is common in English infant schools, recording his work on paper is an established task, then we can add drawing, written communication, and handwriting as talents that are practiced and improved as a result of the box of spools in the corner.

The use of the spools is not limited to one encounter per child. They do not need to be put away until next year's class comes along. The few examples of their use given here might concern a child on a number of occasions over a year or more. In the development of the child, it is a long way from making multicolored towers of spools to designing strings of them in complex patterns and explaining these patterns verbally.

The child's involvement with this flexible set of materials is indicative of the complexity of learning that goes on in infant-school classes. A good teacher is always aware that she is dealing with up to forty distinct children and that at any moment they may be engaged in many different experiences, all equally important.

In the midst of this excitement and exploration, the teacher is naturally concerned with one of the major issues of infant-school teaching—helping the child to begin to read and write. The approaches used in good infant schools are varied and complex.

Learning to read in most English infant schools is

by no means haphazard. Educators and teachers realize that the teaching of reading requires special skill, detailed thought and planning, and a deep understanding of individual children. While teachers seldom fix on any one method as being the right one, most good infant-school teachers are convinced that classrooms run along the lines of those described here are those which will best help the child learn to read. Most of the activities that take place in these classrooms are directly related to the reading process.

One of the teacher's first concerns is with the continuing development of language. Whether the child is painting, engaged in drama, building, or counting, the sensitive teacher makes every attempt to talk with him about what he is doing. A book on infant education by Lesley Webb that is aimed at helping teachers points out the importance of increasing fluency in speech in order to start reading:

> It should be a major task of the infant-school teacher to help children use the spoken word easily and well—and long before they can write and read. . . . Piaget's work has demonstrated to us that words are internalized and are available for use again only insofar as they were, in the first instance, accompanied by action. The adult . . . has to provide opportunities for active involvement and to ensure that appropriate words for the experience are given as the child is engaged in the activity.[3]

The teacher's task in teaching reading is threefold. First, she must establish the atmosphere and materials in the classroom which are conducive to the development of language and individual expression in a variety of forms. Second, she must have planned schemes of reading with which she is comfortable and which are suited to her children. Third, the reading demands that she makes on the children must relate to their particular levels of development. This is a tremendous task.

The example of children's personal writing and reading books illustrates one of the ways that some teachers in England manage to integrate these three goals. In a number of schools the child has a book of about twenty pages, made by the teacher of unlined paper, in which to draw pictures and write. When the child first enters school, he learns that words stand for things. He may be fortunate enough to know a great deal about this already. All the materials in the classroom are clearly labeled. A sign looped over the water tub reads, "Two may play with water." The child's own name appears on a drawer and on his paintings. He must now learn that what he expresses verbally can be represented in words on paper. He quickly begins to paint large pictures, and he expresses many of his ideas and feelings with his paintbrush early in his school career. Talking about the pictures he draws in his book is the next step.

He draws a picture on one side of the page. He and his teacher then talk about it to stimulate his use of descriptive language. If the picture is of a little girl, the teacher may ask the child who she is and where she is. Perhaps they will talk about the tree or cloud in the picture. At first, the teacher may not write anything next to the drawing. But as the child grows accustomed to this kind of work, the teacher will begin to end the discussion by saying, "Now what would you like me to write about the picture?" The child dictates and the teacher writes. The phrases are short and easy to remember: "A little girl," "My house," "A bulldozer." These first phrases are left at the bottom of the page or more often on the facing page. The next day, the teacher may turn back to earlier work and ask if the child remembers what he said. When he does manage to read the words, he is reading from his own prose, using his own vocabulary.

As the child becomes more practiced, his sentences

grow a bit longer. His teacher will suggest that he try to trace over the words she has written for him. When he achieves this, he will move to copying the letters underneath the words she has written. Thus, a girl who had drawn a dark, chaotic picture dictated, "The little girl got run over and she is laying in bed." Seeing the words that she spoke written on the page, she added a number of words to the list of those she could recognize. By copying her teacher's writing, she concentrated on her handwriting and the form of the letters. But most essential, for teacher and child, she was working with words and a subject important to her.

Some children make twelve to fifteen books, copying the words before they are ready to move ahead and write the story on their own. Others move faster through the process. Whatever the case, teacher and child together decide the next step. This joint decision is of major importance to a five- or six-year-old.

When his teacher says, "John, your writing is very nice and you can read a lot of words—what do you think of writing your next story on your own?" it gives John an added sense of responsibility. Whether he agrees to try, or asks to wait for a while, is up to him. The teacher has made a reasonable demand on him, pointing out his achievements so far (better handwriting, stronger vocabulary) and asking him to take another step forward, with her support and help.

Thus, a seven-year-old boy, writing completely on his own for the first time, spent most of the morning on his drawing and then painstakingly wrote, "The wicked witch gets the stewpot ready for the old lady." He carefully referred back to earlier stories to get the words right. His pleasure in finishing the work was enormous, and he was eager to read it to his teacher and his friends.

In addition to building a child's vocabulary and self-confidence, the picture and writing books have many other uses. Friends tend to share their stories with one another. A child looking over someone's shoulder is reading the prose of a friend, written in the same bold if uneven hand that he is familiar with in his own books. The pictures the reader sees are vibrant, colorful images of the writer's story—totally unlike the dry, unfamiliar illustrations of a conventional reader.

The pictures themselves serve many purposes. They allow the younger children to express far more than they ever could if asked to "Tell me a story and we'll write it together," as we have heard teachers say on occasion. They permit everyone to illustrate a good story with visual material to which the children are accustomed through their observation of the world around them.

The pictures form useful aids to reading. The story the child has told is all there in the picture. We saw one six-year-old, a fine writer, stumble over the words "full moon" in reading a story he had written a week before. He turned his attention to his picture, and touching some of the things he had portrayed, looked for the words he needed. For this boy, the tactile experience of tracing the full moon in the drawing was as important as seeing the letters. It was his own method. Low on the horizon he found his moon, returned to his story, and read it through with ease.

By the time children in many English infant schools begin to write, they have substantial dictionaries of their own. In these small booklets the child writes the words he wants to know how to use. He may ask the teacher to spell a needed word, but he will usually have to sound out its initial letter by himself. This provides some training in phonics as well as spelling. It is not unusual to see a group of children working at a table, talking about their stories and occasionally asking one another about spellings. "How do you spell Joseph?" asks one boy of his neighbor. The friend patiently spells it for him, twice, while the boy adds it to his dictionary and then to his story.

In these situations, the child's first books are of his own making. His dictionary is full of words he wanted to learn, not words that his teacher thought he ought to know. This means of learning—evoking words that are vitally important to the child—is very similar to that described by Sylvia Ashton Warner in her book *Teacher,* to which some teachers in England occasionally refer for ideas and support.

Some aspects of these picture-and-writing books are familiar to American teachers. Certainly, writing a child's description of a painting on the sheet of paper is common in most schools. It is the continuity of the work that is striking in English schools, as well as the fact that the books are used for many purposes.

In the best classrooms, the development of individual self-expression is thoroughly integrated with the teacher's overall scheme for teaching reading. Few teachers rely on only one of the commonly accepted methods. Most use a combination of Look-Say and phonics, depending on the kind of words the child is learning.[4] The teacher is constantly teaching reading—but in a style that would not be familiar to many American teachers. The teacher in a good infant school tries to keep close watch on the work of individual children, so that she will know where they are going each day and what steps they need to take next. She will know many of the children's interests and can direct their reading toward them.

The individual teacher does not devise methods for her children in isolation. Many schools feel the need to draw up a broad outline with the cooperation of the staff. This usually includes the basic skills needed for reading, describes various methods and approaches, and discusses the different stages in a child's development. In some schools, there are similar schemes for mathematics. These outlines are never binding, and a teacher is free to work in the best way suited to her class at all times. An outline prepared by the staff as a whole is something for her to refer to and will ensure a degree of continuity throughout the school. The child who moves to a different teacher goes on with the same approach to reading or to math and does not suffer any setbacks. These guidelines also aid new teachers who are unfamiliar with the school's philosophy.

No matter what method the competent teacher employs to help her teach reading, her classroom is likely to testify to an interest in books of all sorts. In addition to storybooks, available in the library corner, there are often a few children's reference books as well as examples of books made by the children singly, in groups, or as a class. The class project book may include stories about the behavior of the class pet. It may tell of a trip or recount an extended study of different kinds of flowers growing near the school. Some class or group efforts discuss mathematical work and are often related to area or measurement. Whatever the content, two or three children often thumb through the pages, reading them aloud to one another. The project book calls upon individual talents in different fields and is personal, since the children themselves do the work. It also illustrates the interdisciplinary nature of the curriculum. A book on flowers, for instance, calls for careful drawing, classification, mathematical work, written descriptions, and the techniques involved in making the book itself.

Copies of publishers' reading schemes appear in the

midst of a profusion of children's writing and good printed books. Many teachers use the schemes as aids to help children who are beginning to read. Some children enjoy them enough to read them on their own. But a large number of teachers to whom we spoke complained, as have American teachers, that conventional readers are dull. Teachers note that the middle-class characters in these books have little relation to the lives of the children in urban areas. The readers remain in use largely as crutches for teachers who lack the knowledge or the confidence to rely more extensively on the children's ability to write and to read what others have written.

The quality of writing that emerges in some infant-school classrooms is astounding. Its spontaneity, wide range of language, and sense of the beauty of words all have their roots in activities which encourage children to think imaginatively and clearly. Many teachers agree that spelling and grammar develop along with this writing. They strive to strengthen the child's confidence and ability to write first and worry about the grammar and spelling as the child progresses. Teachers want the children to see these as tools to make their writing easier to read and understand, not as ends in themselves.

Writing often stems from activities that excite the child. The following example, which we saw on the wall of an infant classroom, describes the process of tie dying. It was written, with minimal aid from the teacher, by two girls who had spent some time dying a large piece of cloth. The cloth and the description, written on a very large piece of paper, hung side by side on the wall.

> We brought some pieces of white material. Diane brought an old pillowcase. Leslie brought an old nurses apron. We tied big knots and little knots. We put string round and round the ma-

terial. We emptied some orange dye into a pan and poured on
1 pint of boiling water. Anne stirred and stirred. We poured 3
jugs of cold water into the pan and then put in our material. It
boiled for 20 minutes.

The beautiful patterns in the cloth testified to the
success of the method they used. The writing showed
their careful attention to the details of the work they
accomplished.

Another story illustrates what can happen when a
child has been encouraged to observe things carefully
and has become aware of movement, sounds, sights,
and smells. It was written while a bulldozer was at work
right outside the windows of the school. The boy quite
unconsciously made his letters bigger and bigger as the
bulldozer got closer to the classroom:

Last Friday two bulldozers
appeared in the field they
started to dig the earth
The earth is heavy and
sticky it is muddy too.
the builders are making
a car park for the big
swimming pool I bet
the Bulldozer picks up
a 100 tons in one day.
Sometimes the tracks
skid becuse the
ground is slippery.
The little Bulldozer
can climb Right over
the heaps of mud
Now the Bulldozer
is shoveling towards
us. It looks like a
YELLOW MONSTER
GOBBLING UPSOIL
WITH ITS BIG
SHARP TEETH

The story was the best writing this six-year-old had done up to the time. His teacher was impressed that the boy had made such fine use of what he had seen to accomplish this writing. The story was mounted and put on display.

Writing such as this indicates that the children's learning in school is not compartmentalized. The story was unsolicited by the teacher and was written at a certain time because the child wanted to write it. The lack of absolute definition allows both teacher and child great freedom to explore the possibilities of anything in which they engage.

In such a setting, we watched the simultaneous learning of reading, writing, spelling, and mathematics take place one afternoon when a small boy undertook a weighing project. He began with a group of conkers (horse chestnuts), which he wanted to compare with various items in boxes near him on the math table.

He first filled one side of a scale with the conkers and watched the scale tip. Then he took a handful of bottle caps and dropped them, one by one, onto the other side of the scale, waiting patiently for the first shift of the balance that would indicate he was close to his goal. When the scale balanced, he carefully counted out the number of bottle caps and the number of conkers and then got out a piece of paper. All through this process, a little girl, one of the youngest in the class, had been watching him and trying to follow his counting.

When he came back with the paper, he drew a picture of the conkers on one side (counting again to test his accuracy) and then of the bottle caps beside them. He began painstakingly to write "ten conkers," checking the spelling on the box where they came from, "balance" (this word was on another child's paper displayed on the wall), and "37 bottle caps."

When he showed his work to the teacher, she asked some questions about the scale and then urged him to balance other objects against the same number of conkers. Back at his table again, he began to experiment with a combination of corks and small buttons. "It will take a lot of these," he remarked to the little girl. But she did not appear to hear, for she was hard at work experimenting at another scale beside him.

The boy's complete absorption was typical of the children's involvement in a number of English schools. To achieve his final results he had called upon his ability to count and to write. He had drawn each of the objects and had written down the total as well. This project demanded that he complete a number of relationships in his mind—the physical objects were represented both pictorially and numerically.

His work involved a kind of thinking often bypassed in schools. The boy could already count well and do some writing. Had he been told just to count things or to do addition problems, he would never have gained as much as he did from this exercise. Similarly, he was not doing conventional weighing to find out how many bottle caps equaled a half pound. The artificial measure would never have held the importance to him that was represented by the two objects he chose to compare.

In addition to the mental effort involved here, it is important to recall this boy's physical acts. He worked delicately with his hands, in ways other than just holding a pencil. He exercised control by carefully placing the bottle caps on the scale, rather than throwing them on to achieve a quick reaction. At the same time, unknown to him, he taught a younger child much about basic counting and weights.

Finally, he had a feeling of accomplishment. He achieved results based on his own ideas and his own choice of materials. The work of this six-year-old was not far removed from playing. Through play, he had first learned how to use the scale, just as the little girl who had watched him was beginning to do.

In many schools in America and some in England, the word "play" still connotes something done in a Friday afternoon free period or an activity engaged in at home. Yet, in most English infant schools, the separation between work and play is almost nonexistent, just as it was for the child when he was learning through play within his own family. What adults call play is a serious experience for the child, and for this reason, infant classrooms present the children with many opportunities to combine play with learning. The description of the spools, given above, is an example of one variety of play. The Wendy House is another.

Found in almost every classroom, the Wendy House, or home corner, is usually three or four pieces of plywood set up as walls, with a door and windows. The walls are high enough so that the children cannot see over them. In varying degrees of refinement, the house is often equipped with costumes, handbags, tea cups, firemen's hats, and a host of other objects added to the collection from time to time.

The Wendy House is a center of great activity, and it is not unusual for a group of children to emerge from it to parade through the class, girls clomping in high-heeled shoes, engrossed in a game of role playing which is helping them to build up relationships with other children. In addition, the house allows the children to move from reality to fantasy and back within the classroom.

Many classrooms have a play shop, often a converted

Wendy House, which the children supply with home-made grocery boxes and real boxes and cans supplied by mothers. In these shops, serious mathematical computation accompanies the buying and selling of goods.

In most infant-school classrooms there is a good collection of building blocks and sometimes of wooden toys. These can prove very important in the development of small motor skills—particularly coordination of the hands and fingers. Blocks and toys also allow the child to invent shapes, buildings, railroads, towers, and so on, and put them to work.

Teachers feel that water play is very important in infant classrooms. Children can experiment with different containers and concepts of volume, conservation, and quantity. Working around a water tub, and the comparable sand trough, children gain much of the knowledge that will help them to understand mathematics when they begin to work with figures on paper.

Another form of play that can become serious business is cooking. Almost every new school has at least one electric stove installed for the use of the children. Working with their own teacher, an aid, or a mother volunteer, groups of boys and girls produce a variety of breads, cakes, and cookies. The recipes are simple, but all demand some computation and cooperation within the group. Cooking proves to be great fun for a number of children—and is particularly satisfying when a batch of good cookies comes out of the oven at the right moment to be shared around the class at recess.

The work that infant-school children do in the arts is also indicative of the close relationship of play with learning. Again, there is little or no separation in the teacher's mind or in the child's between what in America has been called creative activities and learning activities, or work. The lives and interests of the children, combined with the personality of the teacher and the inherent interest of the materials, are all conducive to creative work and behavior in many different areas. As we have already pointed out in the case of the child learning to read, early drawings and pictures may be the source of first written words as well as being spontaneous art work in themselves.

Painting with bright colors and big brushes is a natural activity in the classroom. On a bright, warm day the children often paint outside (if the space is provided), using the colors and sights around them as models. Many infant-school teachers also encourage attempts to sketch or paint given objects accurately, but this is not done at the expense of the child's self-expression and is usually reserved for the older infant-school children.

In one class, a girl brought a drawing of a tree to her teacher, who said kindly, "That's a nice tree, Angela, but I think something is wrong down at the bottom, where the roots go into the ground. Go outside and have a look at that tree by the fence—make your drawing as much like that tree as you can." This suggestion to Angela took some important facts into account: the teacher knew that Angela, an older child, was capable of drawing a tree which was more than a lollipop conception of a stick with a round ball on top. The teacher recalled that she and Angela had not talked about accurate representation for a while and that to make such a suggestion would probably not inhibit Angela's expressive painting in the future.

Art work of this sort may also be combined with a larger project. The child who finds a caterpillar on the way to school may try to draw him accurately and then become interested in writing about his movements, in timing his crossing of a table, or in reading about caterpillars in a book. In many of these classrooms, it becomes impossible to separate art from the continuous flow of activities that take place during the day.

Children are not always involved in work that strikes one as unusual, even in the best infant-school classrooms. Concern over a tree or a caterpillar does not crop up at the right moment every day. Over in a corner, there may be some six-year-olds with pencils and paper, doing arithmetic problems. Their work is likely to be taken from a collection of math cards—pieces of cardboard, sometimes covered with plastic. Some pages are from workbooks and contain traditional math problems, while others suggest experiments in measuring, weighing, and judging directions and distances. While some cards are very standard, others are adaptable and allow for individual learning. A card which has five multiplication problems using the four table asks the child to do more than repeat the answers from memory. In many infant schools, there is no effort to force the child to memorize tables of any sort. Rather, teachers express the hope that the child will experiment with mathematical ideas. He may stack colored tiles in piles of four, counting as he stacks, to solve 6×4. He may see patterns emerge from his work and continue beyond the problems on the cards. Most teachers encourage children to use objects as counting aids, so that buttons, acorns, colored tiles, and spools are as important in a classroom as the manufactured Cuisenaire Rods or Dienes Blocks.[5]

In one school, a poster on the wall asked the child to find the length and width of the room, using whatever form of measurement appealed to him. Different children chose their feet, hands, a trundle wheel, a yardstick, and even a chain of spread-eagled classmates to find an answer.

An example of how far infant-school children can carry mathematical thought comes from a classroom in Leicestershire. The teacher had put a box of flat shapes on a table and asked a group of children to classify them in some way. Most divided them into squares, circles, and triangles, words which they knew already. The children were interested in the words, so the teacher wrote them out on cards, and the children put them in place. The next day a boy brought in a small rectangular box and asked if it was a square. This set off a discussion about the similarities between two- and three-dimensional shapes, or flat shapes and box shapes as the children put it. More and more three dimensional objects arrived in the room.

When we observed this classroom, a six-year-old girl was studying the words "sphere," "rectangle," "solid," and "cube," and finding shapes to match. It was clear that she was doing this because it was tremendously interesting to her.

"If I hadn't seen this happen," said the teacher, "I would never have imagined the children would be interested in geometric forms, much less in learning all the names and relating them to the shapes."

A traditional workbook, filled with page after page of math problems or exercises in any subject, could never achieve the effect of this sort of activity. Yet the workbook is tempting.

"Sometimes," said a teacher in London, "I am dying to write a lot of problems on the board and tell them all to sit down at once and do them—because it would be easier for me. I could relax a bit and keep them very quiet. But now that I've seen how much more they learn when they work individually and how much better I understand where each child is and what his needs are, I could never go back to the old way. It would be terribly unfair."

CHAPTER THREE

Grouping Children in Schools

INTERACTION BETWEEN CHILDREN is a great asset to learning—a fact which is proven by a number of schools in England. Teachers in many parts of the country have found ways of grouping the children which foster cooperative learning. These schemes of grouping cut across age ranges and ability. They reveal many of a teacher's strongest convictions about children and can begin to affect a child the moment he first comes to school.

The curious law and regulations that govern entrance to the English infant school make it possible for children to start school at various ages, depending on the time of year of their birth and how crowded their local schools are. The majority of the children come to school in the term after their fifth birthday. If a child's fifth birthday occurs in February, he might start school that January, when he is four years and eleven months old. If his school is crowded, he may not enter until April. A few education authorities arrange for the children, accompanied by mothers, to visit before the term in which they enter. These are schools which believe they must adapt to the children from the very beginning.

In this setting, a child who is very uncomfortable about school may come only a few days each week until the term after his fifth birthday—when the law requires daily attendance. However, a few schools believe so strongly in the need for flexibility that they violate this law to make a special arrangement for a child with difficulties. In one case, we observed an insecure boy, who had passed his fifth birthday. Throughout the fall, he came to school every morning and went home at lunchtime, even though he was five and a half. When he and his teacher agreed that he was ready to stay for lunch, he extended his day that far. Two weeks later, he was there full time. All this occurred with little fuss and was accepted naturally by the children and their teacher.

A number of schools aid the child's transition from home to classroom with the system of family, or vertical, grouping. This practice places children from the school's entire age range in the same class. Thus, a class of thirty-six children in a vertically grouped infant school might contain about twelve children near the age of five, twelve who are six years old, and twelve near or just above the age of seven.

There are many advantages to this arrangement. The child who comes to school for the first time in September enters a class in which half of the children have been together for nearly a year. There will be children his age and older. On his first day the teacher will have time to work with him and to observe him closely because many of the other children know how to proceed on their own. For some time, he will explore the many opportunities for play that exist in the classroom, sometimes focusing on one thing, then moving quickly from one area to another without any particular concentration. He has time to get to know his teacher, and she him.

It is not unusual to see, in the same classroom, a child who was there the year before working carefully over a drawing and writing a story to go with it, while at the next table a new entrant molds clay. There is no pressure upon the new boy to do what the older children in the class are doing. At the same time, the teacher of a family-grouped class would not be surprised to see the older child break off his work and go talk with the molder of clay, perhaps showing him how to better form a head or an eye, or—and this is more important—getting to know him.

This same older boy may have helped his new classmate to find the labeled drawer where he can store his belongings. The new boy will learn much of the operation of the class from the older children, saving the teacher's time for more important work. The child needs time to become part of the social group in the classroom. He must come to grips with the environment he has entered. He cannot do this if he is faced with a great deal of difficult or incomprehensible work. Nor can he do it in a rigid classroom where contact with other children is held to a minimum, and formal approaches to the teacher alone are the accepted mode.

Family grouping is not developed solely to aid the new child when he enters school. It benefits all the children and their teacher in a number of ways. An important aspect of this grouping is the sense of stability it gives to the child. Under this system, he may have the same class teacher for two or even three years. While some of the children in his class go on to the junior school and some are new, the child will always be with a core of children he has known for some time. He does not face the anxious and confusing change from one class teacher to another at the end of the school year.

Vertical grouping offers many advantages to staff members. The infant-school teacher does not face the terrible strain of coping with thirty-six or even forty children who have never been to school before and who arrive, frightened and uneasy, on the same day in September. More important, vertical grouping establishes continuity in learning. The teacher who can follow each child through two or more years of school is able to watch his progress. She knows his interests, his likes and dislikes. In addition, she knows the stages of development he has achieved and is sure of the next steps he should take. She does not face the frustrations of teachers who are on the verge of success with a child, but never gain it because he leaves at the end of the school year. She can establish deep and understanding friendships with the children and maintain them over a period of time.

Furthermore, it is easier to cope with absences under this system. Although no teacher is happy when children miss school, the child in a family-grouped class does not have to worry about catching up with the others when he comes back. He works at his own rate of speed, and thus takes up his work where he left it.

The benefits of this method have been tested, with positive results. Research at Hereford College of Education and at Manchester College of Education confirms that "[the] lengthened teacher/child relationship revealed more highly integrative relationships in the vertical group and therefore greater emotional security for the children." The same research indicates that vertical grouping promotes better attitudes toward work, ". . . higher levels of aspiration, and. . .less discouragement in failure."[1]

This system of grouping often has its roots in the

village school. Like its counterpart in the United States, the one- or two-teacher school in England was forced to group children in large age ranges. One teacher would be responsible for the children from five to eight years old; the other would work with the older children. In the case of the one-room school, a solitary teacher faced a class that encompassed the whole primary range and some of the secondary years as well. Now many primary schools in both suburban and urban areas of England have found that there is much more to this system than expediency.

A classroom containing children of different ages allows for full individual development. The child sets his own pace for learning, without having to worry about competing with anyone else. Many teachers feel strongly that the child must come to learning in his own way. This belief is reinforced by the growing body of psychological research which stresses that no two children reach the same stage of development at the same time or by the same route. A child of six may understand a mathematical concept that is still confusing to a seven-year-old. The teacher can work with different groups of children according to the level they have reached and the material at hand. She may urge the six-year-old, in this case, to work with the older child on the mathematical concept that is not clear to him. Or she may draw together a number of children who need work in this particular area. The system allows for maximum flexibility.

Family grouping implies a special quality that pervades the classrooms where it is in practice. The relationships among the children are like those in a family in that they encompass a wider and more varied age range. As in many families, the younger children look up to the older ones. They are eager to attain their level of achievement and can learn a great deal from watching their behavior.

The atmosphere in a family grouped classroom is peaceful and productive, busy and relaxed, according to the activities pursued by different groups. The children help each other in many ways. The seven-year-old who takes the new child down the corridor to show him a display on rocks is doing a lot for himself and for the five-year-old beside him. He brings a friend to an exhibit that interests him, a fact that is likely to excite the younger child to enjoy the display. He will share some knowledge about rocks with him. He may look up a rock in a book nearby, and the five-year-old begins to understand that the words in the book relate to the objects on the table. The older boy may read to the younger one, thus getting some practice in reading aloud. They share an experience and begin to talk about the collection. This cooperative learning, across different ages, promotes a spirit of unity in classrooms and teaches the children the value of caring for another.

This system only works if the teacher believes in it and is able to convey this belief to the children. Some infant-school teachers prefer to work with groups that cover only one and a half years in age, rather than three. At the junior level, there are fewer schools which use this method, but those who do often group the eight- and nine-year-olds together as one group and the ten- and eleven-year-olds as another. We did not observe any school which had succeeded in grouping children of the full age range (seven-plus to eleven-plus), except for short periods during the day.

When some form of vertical grouping is carried out at the infant or junior level, it implies an attitude toward children and learning which is entirely different from that in most American schools. The average American six-year-old, coming to the end of first grade, faces two future possibilities. In most cases, he is "promoted" to second grade. The less lucky child, however, fails (or "stays back" or "repeats" the year). All of these terms imply that the teacher or the school measures the child against an established standard. The child's work in the classroom is compared both to this set standard and to the work of his classmates. The school assumes that there is a set body of knowledge that the average six-year-old on his way to second grade should know. If he has not been able to grasp the required work, then he may have to spend another year in the same grade. Undoubtedly, he will repeat the same material the following year. The experience of failure at such an early age can be devastating.

In England, schools that are working along informal lines do not consider the child in terms of promotion or failure. Whether the children are grouped vertically or year by year, the question of promotion based on attainment does not exist. The English once had a strict year by year pass or stay back system, akin to what we see in many American schools. Schools in England abandoned this practice in the 1920's.

Today, the child in the unusual infant or junior school works at his own speed and in a way that is compatible with his temperament, interests, and personality. He measures his progress in terms of his own capabilities. The infant school teacher, for example, will have a broad understanding of the concepts she hopes the child will understand by the time he goes on to junior school. But even if her class contained only six-year-olds, she would never assume that they should all be at the same level at the end of a year with her. She would measure each child's progress in terms of what he had been like at the beginning of the year and what he had accomplished since then. Looking at children in this way gives each child the chance to discover his own worth and to develop fully without the fear of failure.

In a vertically grouped class, this attitude is even more apparent. The child moves along steadily through his years in the infant school or the junior school. He has time for a major step forward—and time to relax and even regress a bit if necessary. There is no external standard that pushes him to compete for the sake of competition. Instead, he moves forward because the work is important to him and because his teacher treats him as an individual with needs that are very different from those of his classmates.

The only drawback to this system is the possibility that a child could be trapped with a poor teacher for two or three years or find himself in a situation where he is incompatible with the teacher. This is a danger that many teachers in England have recognized, and there are a number of ways to deal with it. In the case of incompatibility, schools try to remain flexible enough to shift a child from one class to another if they feel he will fit into a different group more easily, or if the child and his teacher are on bad terms.

The poor teacher is a difficult problem in any school. If the teacher is really terrible, the head teacher will try to have him or her resign or transfer to a nonteaching post. The children, in this case, would move on to another teacher the next year. For the teacher who is on the borderline, but not a failure, there are possibilities open to the head teacher which do not always exist in American schools.

The most successful aid to the mediocre teacher is

the support and assistance that a good head teacher and his staff can provide. The head teacher may devote a great deal of time to aiding the teacher in question. Or he may pair this member of the staff with a better teacher, who can set an example and promote the exchange of ideas. A number of schools find that with more flexible classrooms and the chance for easy communication between teachers the quality of the teaching tends to rise toward those staff members who are the leaders in the building.

Another aid to a teacher with difficulties is the local education authority's advisory system (discussed in Chapter Eight.) An adviser, who is an experienced teacher, can do a great deal to help another teacher who is unsure of methods or approaches in the classroom. In cooperation with schools and other organizations, advisory systems often run a wide variety of workshops and seminars to aid teachers with their work.

With commitment from the staff, teaching can be improved to benefit the children. Positive efforts have been particularly successful in the infant schools, whereas the junior schools have lagged behind.

Regardless of the kind of grouping the child has experienced in his infant school, the first severe division he is likely to face in his schooling is the switch to the junior level. The break between infant and junior schools is an artificial one which occurs throughout England. Many of the seven-year-olds who leave their infant school to move into a new setting are not ready for the change. They may lose a familiar teacher and a classroom geared to their specific needs.

The child who transfers from an infant to a junior school encounters a wide variety of teaching methods and approaches to children. The changes within English state education to a more creative and open experience for children have had their real roots in the infant schools. The teachers of the older children are only beginning to catch up in thought and practice.

There are two important factors which have curtailed forward movement in the junior school. The first concerns its history. Until the publication of the Hadow Report in 1931, children of junior age were the youngest and most neglected members of "all-age" schools for eight- to fourteen-year-olds.[2] Although Hadow recommended the creation of special schools for eight- to eleven-year-olds, and some were opened shortly afterward, general lack of interest in this age continued.

The second obstacle to experimentation and change in junior schools has been the eleven-plus examination, which many areas have now abandoned. This test, taken at the age of eleven, determined the child's secondary experience.

If a student did well on the exam, he went to a grammar school and sometimes on to a university. If he failed the exam, he went to a "secondary modern" school, where education proceeded until the age of fourteen or fifteen. It was difficult for a child to transfer from one type of secondary school to another once the exam had settled his fate. To make matters worse, children were "streamed" in junior schools (that is, divided into classes according to certain abilities). The school separated the children into three or more streams (A, B, C, and so forth) at the ripe age of seven and a half to eight, long before the eleven-plus exam.

An enormous amount of pressure fell on both the children and the teachers, who realized that failure of the exam could mean failure in later life. Classes were extremely competitive and almost entirely teacher-directed. The teacher was expected to take the playful seven-year-old, place him in a regimented environment, and cram him full of knowledge.

The effects of this system are slow to die. There are

still many junior schools in England that practice streaming despite much publicized evidence demonstrating that ability grouping gives no advantage to the bright children while it has an adverse effect on those in the lower streams.[3]

Even in schools where streaming no longer exists, we have occasionally encountered a teacher who is reluctant to abandon the practice. Although he believes that "we no longer stream them here," he will point to a group that is seated together and say in a voice audible to all: "These are my star pupils. Way ahead of all the rest. Grammar school material, you know." This is a far cry from the better classes in which progress is measured in terms of the child's own abilities rather than by a standard set up and broadcast by the teacher.

In general, the change to a more open-ended structure has been facilitated when junior and infant schools occupy the same building under one head teacher. This is the situation most comparable to an American elementary school in terms of age and organization, but it is not a common arrangement throughout England. In some areas, two distinct schools, run by two heads, occupy the same building. Elsewhere, the infant and junior schools are entirely separate. Whether or not the schools are physically attached, they are almost always distinct units. Children are aware that they are "going up" to the juniors, even if it only means crossing the hall.

The most common difficulty for the seven-year-old who moves into this new setting lies in the learning of reading. A child who enters junior school is often expected to read well in his first months there, and many children do. Some, however, are just on the verge of becoming competent readers as they leave the infant school. The move to a new school and a different teacher sets them back. The junior-school teacher often feels less responsible for reading. He may not have been exposed to the teaching of reading at his college of education.[4] A number of junior teachers, faced with some children who are behind in reading, are annoyed with the previous teacher. Some say bitterly, "We expect them to come to us knowing how to read and write so we can get on with the work we were trained to do."

If the teacher at the junior level attempts to teach reading, he may do it in a way that is utterly foreign to the child. This is further evidence of the need for better communication between many infant and junior schools.

A similar problem exists in America when children transfer from first to second grade or from second to third grade. In these moves, the child often meets different methods of teaching reading at a time when continuity and encouragement are most needed. In England, the system of family grouping alleviates this problem, for usually the child will be exposed to an approach to reading which is continuous and thought out in advance. Schools which do not practice this method often try to work out an overall scheme for the school, as we mentioned in Chapter Two. But the transition from infant to junior school often takes too little notice of this careful planning.

The Plowden Report was very concerned with the problems of transfer from the infant to the junior level. It is worthwhile to note here what the Plowden Committee recommended as a solution:

> Many infant schools are outstanding for the quality of the relationships between teachers and children. They excel in the opportunities they provide for play and the talk that accompanies it, the stress they put on individual learning and the skill with which teachers select from the various methods of teach-

ing reading those that suit themselves and the individual children.

Two years is too short to profit fully from these qualities of the good infant school.

We conclude, therefore, that children should have three years in the infant school and that they should not transfer until the age of eight.[5]

This recommendation is not yet general policy, but some schools are trying to act upon the idea. Most children still leave the infant school at about seven and a half. Despite the difficulties of this change, mentioned above, the new junior school child has the advantage of working and living in a fairly small school building that he can explore without fear. He will go into a junior school grouped either by age or possibly by a system of vertical grouping.

In the majority of the junior schools in England, the staff has not discussed any alternative method for grouping children other than the standard practice of moving the children through schools on a year by year basis. The child in most junior schools passes through four age-grouped years, just as he would pass through grades in the United States. If he is extremely lucky, his will be a school that has devised an excellent atmosphere for children and staff, a school that has taken account of the good work that has gone on for so many years at the infant level.

CHAPTER FOUR

Days with Juniors

IN A FEW JUNIOR SCHOOLS the switch to a more child-centered setting has stimulated a change in attitudes toward learning. Rather than attempting to impose the same set of facts and amount of knowledge on each child, teachers are concerned that their pupils develop new ways of thinking. They seek to extend the powers of observation and inquiry which the children bring with them from infant school. Charity James, a respected English educator, says of good primary schools: "These are schools where it is not for the child to find out what the teacher wants and give it to him, but for the teacher to observe what the child is becoming and help him to find out what he needs."[1]

Junior schools which think creatively about their students provide both a challenging and rigorous setting. Pupils undertake a great deal of hard work and attain a startling degree of excellence. The pride of accomplishment that these children show in their finished work is a joy to see, and it is important to note that this is usually work they have initiated and brought to fruition themselves, with the aid of their teacher.

We visited a large classroom in a junior school which illustrated the variety of work that can take place in one room. Six children grouped at a long table were making their conceptions of American Indian ritual masks out of paper, bits of cloth, and flexible reeds. The idea for the masks came from discussions and readings on Indians. Members of the class planned to use them in a dance later that week. The careful work of the maskmakers did not disturb a group gathered with a teacher at a round table. They had been reading some poetry written by members of the class and were talking about ideas for new poems.

Around the corner in this large room, other children were studying a collection of bones. A number of different animal skeletons had arrived on loan from the museum service. Some children were making accurate drawings of them; others searched through reference books to identify the original owners. ("Look, John, it's a mole, that's what it is!")

Still others handled the skeletons, running their fingers across a delicate structure or looking at it from many angles. Two girls wrote about the sheep's skull that lay on the table in front of them. All these children were talking, discussing, and thinking out loud about bones, animals, shapes. A typical reaction: "OOOh, that's ugly. Think of a rabbit looking so ugly underneath!"

A boy at work near a window was building a scale model of a suspension bridge. He worked with papier-mâché, wood, wire, and other materials. This delicate task required a good deal of mathematics and a lot of reading. Open before him was an encyclopedia and a text on bridges. Why had he started this lengthy job?

"I saw the new bridge over the Severn River and I wanted to make a model of it."

The sight of the bridge, on a weekend drive, initiated the thinking that resulted in a complex project. This ten-year-old's teacher had urged him to go deeper and deeper into the subject and to make as accurate a model as he could. The teacher told us he would not consider diverting the boy from the work. Making the model of the bridge had posed challenging mathematical problems, and the boy had thrown himself into some difficult reading and was culling from it the information that was applicable to the design. This was not the mindless copying of paragraphs for a report, which we see so often with children of this age.

This remarkable variety of work took place at once in a large classroom. For most of the time, there were thirty-seven children in the room with one teacher. Scenes of this nature are common in those few junior schools where the work is rooted in human needs and interests. Someone coming into these classrooms for a few moments might be alarmed that some children talked in a group in a corner, that others were painting and said they had been painting all morning, and that one child reported he had not done any math since two days before. Yet the children pursue and achieve excellence in many areas.

These junior schools have not organized their working days in any standard fashion. There are great differences, both from class to class and within the same room on different days. On any one day, children may come into a class and set to work on a task begun the day before while others will consult their teacher about work to be done or a new idea. A third group of children may like to begin their day by dealing with the chores of the classroom, cleaning the animal cages, and getting out special equipment. Tomorrow the membership of each group will probably be substantially different.

No class could ever work in this informal way and be successful if the teacher had to indicate the direction each child's work was to take every day. The teacher must respect the children's ideas and allow them to act upon them. This, in turn, permits the teacher to give his time where it is most needed, to children with immediate problems. Some children may finish a sequence of work and ask for advice on their next project. Others may have come to school depressed and in need of help. Family difficulties, an argument with a friend—anything may come into the open between child and teacher and lead to a discussion.

A whole class of thirty to forty children seldom does a specific thing at a set time in a school run this way. It is not unusual, however, for a teacher to bring the group together in order to discuss new materials, suggest new ways to approach a particular problem, or talk about the work that some children have completed. As was the case with the boy who built the model of the Severn Bridge, a teacher may allow a child to work for an extended period on one project, often skipping regular tasks, such as math, and sometimes ignoring meetings with the rest of the class. The good teacher seldom tries to lure a child back to any mainstream of work in the classroom, but attempts instead to extend and vary the child's interest within a range of subjects. The group that made the Indian masks, for example, went on to a further understanding of dance, ritual, and some of the history of American Indian tribes. They read extensively, wrote about aspects of what they had learned, and then combined it all in dance and drama using the masks, their own creations.

Because children in a few good junior schools often

work from week to week, rather than day to day, it is nearly impossible to describe the typical day for a child of this age. Instead, the following examples illustrate the work undertaken by groups of children in one class over the course of three or four weeks.

These children were all younger juniors (eight- and nine-year-olds.) At the beginning of the spring term, their teacher set up a display of yellow and gold items in a corner of the classroom. At the center of the display was a large bolt of cloth, which the teacher had tie dyed a startling bronze color. The material dominated one large corner of the room and seemed to magnify the sunlight that streamed in through the window. The dying created enormous white swirls in different parts of the cloth. On one of the first days of the term, the teacher talked with the children about the colors in the exhibit and how the gold was repeated in the shocks of wheat, photographs, and other yellow objects clustered near the cloth. Many children said that the display reminded them of sunlight and that the swirls in the material were like the sun.

Others concentrated on the gold color. They were reminded of Greek myths, and they heard the story of the Golden Fleece, Medusa, and Icarus, whose flight took him too close to the sun.

After further discussions, the class wrote a joint, impressionistic piece which included many of their thoughts on the display:

> yellow is a light a burning sun
> shining on the corn
> it is a leaf in autumn, golden
> on the ground
> A heap of yellow fruit,
> lemons, bananas, melons,
> yellow is bees collecting pollen and
> making honey.

yellow is a leaping tiger
a fish of brass.
it is a flaming fire or a cornish
ice cream on a hot day.
Yellow is a sandstorm
or shy daffodils a stabbing beak
a singing bird.
The colour of deep summer.

Following this effort, a number of children went on to write their own stories or poems.

Two girls in the class had different ideas about the display. They had immediately noticed that the circles in the cloth on the wall were like enormous eyes, and they asked the teacher if they might try to make some out of blue dye. With the teacher's help, they tie dyed two blue and white "eyes" on a piece of cloth, cut them out in the proper shape, mounted them, and framed them with paper lashes. The eyes, when mounted on the wall, were about two feet across and a foot high. Their dark "pupils" were piercing and seemed capable of sight.

The girls began to think about sight itself, and asked their teacher where they might find some real eyes to examine. They obtained a few frogs' eyes, which they dissected, drew, and wrote about:

The frog's eyes bulge out of his
head. He has no eyelashes.
Round his eye where the pupil is
he has a ring of gold. On a
human eye it is called an iris.
The rest of the eye is black.
It is joined to the head with a
strip of skin that reaches from the
head to the hind legs.

Their next interest was the human eye, which they read about, drew, and studied for some time. This project, beginning with the tie dying and ending with the human eye, absorbed them for three or four weeks. At the same time, they carried on with more conventional work in mathematics and reading.

Meanwhile, other members of the class branched off into different topics, all stimulated by the original discussion about sunlight and the stories of Jason, Icarus, and Medusa. A group interested in the monsters described in the myths began to talk about snakes, and their teacher brought a live one to school. This led to drawings of snakeskin, research on reptiles, and further work with frogs, toads, and newts. Some children built a vivarium to house the pet grasssnake.

The tale of Icarus and his sad flight excited two other groups of children. Some were interested in the flight itself, wanting to know if Icarus really did fly and what allows birds and planes to leave the earth. They constructed models of a hot-air balloon and an airship, both involving mathematics and scale drawings.

A second group of boys was concerned about the ending of the myth, when Icarus flies too close to the sun, causing the wax on his wings to melt. They began to discuss the sun and its proximity to earth. The head teacher, hearing of this interest, brought in a book about the sun and encouraged some of the children to begin a study of the solar system.

They started with a flat diagram of the planets. After long hours of mathematical figuring, they worked out a chart that showed the planets' sizes to scale. They also did some reading and wrote a brief description of each planet. The teacher then urged them to try bigger, three-dimensional figures to show relative distances as well as accurate size. This they did, using papier-mâché to make the models. They read further about the planets so that they could paint their models accurately.

They then hung them from the ceiling on fishing line, using a distance scale of one centimeter to one million miles. Their classroom was just long enough to accommodate this distance, from the flat paper sunburst they had made on the wall to the tiny, three-dimensional Pluto hanging at the other end of the room. When we saw the planets on display, hanging at the proper distances, the boys had yet another project in mind: they planned to work out a distance scale of ten thousand miles to the inch—which would take them beyond the school playground to the outskirts of town. The teacher hoped this would help them imagine the enormous distances in the solar system.

In all of these projects—the study of eyes, flight, and the exploration of the solar system—the teacher was directly involved. While he did not force these children to undertake their projects, he encouraged them to continue, throwing in new ideas when interest in one aspect failed. He was there to help one group with some very difficult math and to show the girls how to dissect the eye. He had sparked these interests with his original display and worked with the class as a whole before allowing them to take off on their own. As with so many junior projects in good schools, the children worked in a variety of ways—some prefered to work alone, others with a partner, while the boys studying the solar system formed a larger group.

At one point, the teacher consolidated many different activities by bringing the group together for a brief period. The children sat around the room facing the tie-dyed eyes. The teacher played a record of a piece of music called "The Planets" and asked the children to look into the eyes as they listened to it. At the end of the record, the pupils wrote about the feelings evoked by the experience. One child's impression was as follows:

> The blue eyes stare at me. They never
> look away. They make me scared.
> The pupils look like blazing
> fires.
> They burn into me.
> The eyelashes seem to pull me towards
> them, like a powerful magnet
> I try to run
> The eyes are too strong for me
> I can hardly take a step
> I saw a pit.
> Two more eyes were coming
> out of the pit.
> I fell to my knees and
> crawled to a pond.
> There was an old bucket there
> I got some water in it and
> threw water at one of the eyes
> The eyes disappeared.
> I threw water at the other
> eyes. They disappeared
> all their power had gone.
> Then I ran home.

Aspects of these projects gave the child the sort of experience that Charity James feels is so greatly needed throughout the school years:

> How much more profitable productive and critical thinking would be if it were demanded by the nature of the child's engagement, that is if the need for rigour arose from the creative purpose rather than the apparently arbitrary decision of the teacher; if the answer to the question, "Why are you doing that?" were not, "Because I was told to," or "Because we always do," but "Because I need to," whether the need is to test a hypothesis, to make one's dancing more skilful and expressive, or to get a pot ready for firing.[2]

Although James directs her comments toward secondary school, primary education must foster this kind of thinking as early as possible. For the child to be in a position to reply "Because I need to," his own needs must be the cornerstone of his entire school experience.

Most junior schools in England have not yet carried their children to this level of thinking. A few, however, have reached it by building on the successes of the infant schools. In many other areas, teachers would like to approach the children this way, but are not sure how to go about it.

It does not appear that we are close to this kind of work in the overall curriculum of American elementary schools. In isolated instances, "Because I need to" might be heard. It is a reply that could accompany some work based upon an Elementary Science Study unit, for example, but there is seldom a carryover from work in one subject or project to include the child's work in other areas of the curriculum.[3] The work we describe throughout the rest of this chapter illustrates how a small number of schools have attempted to deal with the junior child's complete experience in learning.

EXPLORING THE SENSES

Sense experience . . . provides the raw material for reflection. . . . This work demands a rather special viewing of the classroom environment. We seek to entice, to fascinate, to encourage children to look into the heart of things. We want them to listen more carefully, look more closely and touch more sensitively.[4]

In the best English schools, junior children engage in a variety of activities that are sensory in nature. The descriptions that follow represent a few of the many ways that children and their teachers grow in their perceptions of themselves and each other as they explore the world around them.

We witnessed one aspect of sensory experience in an Oxfordshire school where different shapes, textures, and designs evoked varying responses in the children. An exhibit of metals was on display in a junior classroom. About fifteen children were eagerly handling and examining the items, each child absorbed by different aspects of the material. There were jugs, pitchers, plates of pewter, and iron implements for cooking, farming, and hand crafting. Objects of tin, brass, and copper stood on the display table. Some were complete items, others fragments that might or might not be identifiable.

The children who held the samples rubbed them, studied them, and talked about them with a neighbor. Some children were making careful, detailed drawings of the pieces they liked, using pencil first for accuracy. Others were more concerned with mathematical aspects of the display and spent time weighing and measuring particular pieces. A small group was clustered around the teacher, deep in a discussion about the strengths of different metals.

One child wrote about the texture, color, and size of a lovely brass pitcher. He used paper and pencil with the specific aim of recording the acute observations he had made. He hoped to describe the pitcher so that a person who had not seen it would gain an accurate image of it by reading about it. A girl by the window was concerned with the more emotive qualities of a twisted and pitted piece of iron which looked, she said, "like the arm of a monster."

The display of metals had been in the classroom for only a few days, and many children were just beginning to explore the materials. In the best junior classes, a child often involves his whole self in the work at hand. Much of his personality and feelings are revealed to the teacher as he creates a pottery bowl, makes a pattern of potato printings on a curtain, or writes about the piece of iron in his hand. The interaction of the teacher with the child is vital.

It is the teacher who makes an initial selection of materials, which either intrigue or bore the children. It is the interest of the teacher in the materials and in what the child is doing that encourages work of outstanding quality. The teacher's recognition of the needs of a particular child allow him to help the pupil toward a manner of working that is totally involving.

A friend teaching in Leicestershire described to us the dramatic change that took place in a boy who brought his rock collection, made outside school, into the classroom. While he had once been reticent and withdrawn from activities, this act of bringing an essential part of himself into the school transformed his relationships with the children. They were intensely interested in his collection and his knowledge. His teacher gained a new basis for working with him.

Many teachers can remember children bringing something of great importance into the classroom, but how many can say they seized upon this event to draw a part of the child's outside life into school? It is one of the accomplishments of some English schoolteachers that they often manage to do this. Both the philosophy behind their teaching and the freedom of the school day encourages them to draw upon the special interests of one or more of the children.

Sometimes, the skills of the teacher will mesh with the interests of a group of children to provide a tremendously exciting working situation within a classroom. We witnessed such an event in a small village school where a new teacher had just arrived, bringing with her an enthusiasm for weaving and for unusual art effects. Her excitement caught the imagination of the children—a group of juniors who already had experience in the use of natural materials in art. Their common interests led to a number of different projects.

The class had previously studied some of the farm animals in the region with the head teacher. As part of their study of sheep, they collected samples of wool from barbed-wire fences and hedges, with little follow-up in the classroom. Now, with their new teacher, they planned to gather more wool and then to card, spin, and weave it, using dyes at different times to achieve particular effects. Although the teachers in the school could have dealt with weaving as simply one activity in a crafts period, they saw that their own interests and the interests of the children permitted a broader approach.

The children were engaged in all the mechanical and physical acts needed to transform the raw wool into finished fabric, and also asked questions about its history. Why were there certain towns with areas called wool markets in them, even though no one sold wool there now? The children came to these issues through their own natural curiosity and the sensory experiences of actually handling and working with the wool. Other children were more taken with the equipment involved in weaving than with the wool itself. Three boys gathered around the loom to talk and grew interested in its workings. Their teacher noticed them and brought over a pamphlet on building looms. For nearly an hour, they were engrossed in the book and the loom in front of them.

The teachers in this school made no special demands on the class as a whole. Most of the children worked very hard on weaving or subjects related to it. Some chose to use other materials, not connected to wool or weaving. Despite the skill of the new teacher in weaving and the interest of the head teacher who worked with her, neither would have chosen to coerce a child who was diligently engaged in something else to join the rest of the group.

We saw a different approach to the same subject at an Oxfordshire school. A group of children had decided to assemble some extensive displays about wool and what could be done with it. This exhibit formed as large a project as working with the wool itself. The children passed through many stages in dealing with the wool. They collected it from hedgerows, then washed it, carded it, and used two distinct methods to spin it. They experimented with a number of exciting dye techniques. A group collected natural materials (beets, elderberry, onionskin) and made dyes from them. At the end of the process, the wool was never quite the color the children had expected, leading them to investigate the chemical sources of color in the materials they had used.

The finished display included wall posters that explained the qualities of certain colors and the natural method of obtaining them. Shanks of dyed wool hung near the posters to illustrate the points. Two girls sat on a low bench, below the posters, weaving a necktie from wool that they had prepared from its beginnings on the fences in the neighborhood. They were interested in the aesthetic qualities of the colors they were using, the feel of the material as it progressed from wool to cloth, and the patterns made as they passed the shuttle back and forth.

As one might expect, a number of children in this class were involved in completely different activities. Four or five children, seated around a table, were drawing some pussy willows the teacher had brought in that morning. Now and then, a finger passed over the soft buds as a child studied their form carefully. On the walls of the classroom, in addition to the wool display, were recently completed examples of multicolored tie dying. Substantial painting took place at different times in this room and very graphic writing accompanied and complemented all the work.

Perhaps the most important feature of sensory experiences such as these is the way they can develop unity in learning. The child learns to use his hands, his ears, his eyes, and his mind with equal proficiency. Unfortunately, only the best teacher is able to ensure that every child will have the chance to explore all the available areas of sensory experience. Yet it is remarkable how many teachers have encouraged their children to look at objects with great care and record what they see with imagination and skill, whether in writing, movement, or drawing.

The children have also begun to listen more carefully —although this is an area where many teachers could make further efforts. Music is sorely neglected in many schools, especially at the junior level. While a number of infant schools arouse children's interest in music with simple instruments, such as those designed by the musician Carl Orff, teachers in the junior schools are often unable to help the children to a more advanced level. The exceptions are local authorities, such as the West Riding of Yorkshire, which provide the schools with peripatetic teachers of music. These men and women are helping to fill the gap, but they need more assistance from the schools themselves.

We saw one instance where a teacher had coordinated music with other activities. His pupils made their own instruments, composed simple tunes, and filled their room with the sounds of recorders, xylophones, and other percussive instruments. In another small village school, every child from the age of five to eleven was able to play some instrument. This type of experience will gain in frequency only as hesitant teachers attend classes and workshops and find that they can be musicians.

The education of teachers has been essential to the development of more varied experiences for children. The best example is in the art that many children produce as juniors. The children are able to fire a pot or make an interesting collage only because their teacher has learned to appreciate art and has himself gained the ability to produce something worthwhile with his hands.

Art and the work it stimulates are very impressive in some junior schools. An observer expects to see excellent art work in infant classrooms. Many countries, the United States included, accept and encourage artistic expression in young children. We expect to see children painting in the first two or three grades of school and would be surprised to find a teacher who forbade it. But often, as American children reach the higher elementary grades, the amount of art work declines, sometimes to nil. This was once true in many English schools, and still is in some areas. But today, many teachers in England believe that art can form an integral part of the whole primary experience.

A good junior school teacher regards art as a means to enhance the work of the children in many fields. Such a teacher will try to lead the children into many varieties of art work. In the best schools, where a few teachers are proficient in one area or another, the children have access to many different media. Pottery, silk screening, prints made from wood or linocuts—all are a part of life in many exciting classrooms. The children will be encouraged to draw and sketch in detail as well as to paint large, expansive pictures. In some areas, handwriting is itself an art form. A child may make a book that involves many different methods of work. He will compose his own poems or stories, copying them neatly onto clean sheets of paper in his best handwriting. He will illustrate his work and then go on to make a cover for the book from material he has printed and dyed, or perhaps from a wood block he has perfected over the last few weeks.

The sensory experiences of working with art thus relate to more conventional school work. In one school, a class spent a few days talking about the Middle Ages. A group of ten- and eleven-year-olds became intrigued with illuminated writing practiced in the monasteries. Although they were unable to get to a museum where examples might be on display, they found some photographs in a number of books and began their own experiments. They revised and copied a report on some of the houses in their town. The margins and the first letter or word of each paragraph were enlarged and illuminated. A school report became a work of art. With the encouragement of their teacher, this group of children had explored an important part of the Middle Ages and had gone beyond mere historical curiosity to test out this art form with their own work.

The children whose work we discuss here have looked "into the heart of things," as Leonard Marsh suggests that they must. The work that we describe formed an important portion of these children's school experience. Each child reacted to these different activities in his own way. The sensory experiences they engaged in appeared to provide, from all we have been able to learn, valuable raw material for reflection which enhanced much of the rest of their efforts in school.

Teachers in English junior schools are faced with a difficult job. They are concerned with the excellence of both the specific pieces of work the children undertake and the caliber of their learning and development at the time they leave the school at the age of eleven. These teachers do not look upon their classroom methods as ends in themselves. They are valid only if the work is clearly beneficial to the children. Many teachers feel that an essential part of the learning process is the ability to communicate effectively with others. Some try to guide much of the work in the classroom toward this end. They argue that if a child has written poetry or practiced a piece of music, he can gain a great deal from the appreciation or criticism of his friends. For this reason, discussion takes place all the time in many classrooms. The child who looks over his friend's shoulder to comment on the accuracy of a drawing is helping the artist while increasing his own sense of how the work of another child differs from his own. Teachers often lead discussions that show the children, indirectly, the value of positive criticism as opposed to silly comments. The atmosphere of cooperation in a good classroom is of particular importance to this sort of talk.

Another very important way of sharing work is through displays of the finished product. Whether the walls are hung with paintings, poems, block prints, silk screening, poetry, descriptions of experiences, or complex geometric designs, the displays share a common characteristic in many of the best schools: they are of exceptional quality and reflect the degree of excellence achieved by the child on a certain piece of work. This does not mean that the same standard applies to all the children. The teacher must take differing abilities into account. If he is sensitive, he is careful to see that everyone is represented often in the changing exhibits. In some schools, children mount and prepare these displays themselves. In too many others, the teacher still does the finishing work, detracting from the child's overall feeling of accomplishment and pride.

The achievement of excellence is individual, and the best junior-school teachers emphasize their belief that there is no set standard which applies to every child. The teacher will, however, demand that the child do his best and that his work show a reasonable amount of improvement during the year. The idea that the children can improve upon and refine their own work is a valuable thought for them to grasp at this age. We had an opportunity to see children gain this sort of understanding in a school where a class had heard about the Norman invasion of England and where one group of children decided to pursue the topic further.

These children were interested in the way the Normans had become a part of the island and combined their way of life with that of the English. They began to do some reading, but soon tired of the books available. It was dry reading, which answered only a few of their questions. They sought a more direct way to approach the subject.

These nine-year-olds, working independently from the rest of their class, decided to build a model of a Norman village of the type that might have existed in their area. They collected the materials themselves. They received advice from teachers who knew something of model building. The job took a number of weeks, but when it was done they had completed a strikingly accurate, three-dimensional cardboard, wood, and styrofoam model of the main street of such a town.

The details of each house were made to scale, involving extensive mathematics. The research had taken them far beyond the histories they had first read. The building and painting of the model required great manual dexterity. The team devoted far more care and time to this than they would have to any one painting or bit of woodwork that they might otherwise have worked on during those days. The model itself was of high quality and expressed, better than a teacher's grade ever could, the amount of care, involvement, and hard work that had gone into its construction. The excellence of this particular project, however, was not limited to the model making.

The children had also been drawn toward some writing. What they wrote was not a common report assigned by their teacher, but a series of papers on topics that had come to mind as a result of their work. Some sketched the history of Norman towns with facts gleaned from reading. Other children put themselves in the midst of their model, writing stories of themselves in their village. The children first did their writing without too much concern for grammar and spelling, but with a desire to get their ideas on paper. Once this was done, they showed their work to the teacher, who helped them with the technical side of the writing.

Aside from the generally high quality of this writing, it was impressive to see that the children using books for research had not copied material directly from the books, a problem that is common in more formal primary-school classrooms in England and the United States. Apparently, the experience of building the model and talking about their work had given them the confidence to be critical of what they read and the desire to put on paper exactly what they felt to be true, even when they were in disagreement with a book. They had broken through the barrier that so many children face of believing that what is in print cannot be contradicted and therefore might just as well be copied.

In outstanding junior schools, words that once helped to divide the curriculum (reading, spelling, history, geography, science) are losing their usefulness. Neither the boy who built the model of the Severn Bridge nor his teacher thought of his work as being divided into crafts, reading, mathematics, engineering, and geography—though he made use of each of these fields in completing his work. He was prepared to study any discipline that would help him to complete the bridge as he envisioned it. Yet, despite examples such as this, parts of the curriculum in many schools remain compartmentalized.

All teachers are concerned with the competence of their children in reading and mathematics. Historically, these two subjects have been taught independently, and in the bulk of English schools, math is still a separate subject. Reading, on the other hand, is only a distinct subject when it involves remedial work. A common approach to reading in quite a few junior schools is to integrate it as much as possible with other work. Reading is a pleasurable activity when the content is attractive to the child.

In the West Riding of Yorkshire, we talked to a ten-year-old girl who had become intrigued by the fact that some objects floated on water while others sank. She had noticed that of two, apparently similar, large crayons, one sank to the bottom of a tub of water while the other floated. Her teacher urged her to read two short science books about water, the density of objects, and the problems of getting a heavy object to float by designing it to do so. With the help of her teacher and a dictionary, she read the books carefully, improving her reading skills and vocabulary in the process. Fortunately, the school provided her with the proper books and with the facilities to experiment with flotation as she read.

She found a large plastic basin, filled it with water, and collected a number of different materials and objects to test, keeping notes as she did so. Her work, carried out in the classroom while other work was going on, caused no disturbance to the rest of the class. It did, however, draw some of her friends over to her corner to observe her work for a few minutes and get a glimpse of a problem they perhaps had not thought about before. Her work in one aspect of physics led her to pursue reading not as an end in itself, but for the explicit purpose of studying a subject that was important to her.

In other cases, where teachers strive to make reading a pleasurable activity, the school library plays an important role, as does the collection of reading books in each classroom. Head teachers of junior schools often devote substantial amounts of their budget to buying books, and although there are never enough, most schools have on hand a reasonable selection on varied subjects, aimed at different levels of reading competence. In a school run on informal lines, children can seek out books at many times during the day. They can visit the library if the school has one or ask in another class for a book they need. Collections of books are in greater demand and more extensively used in this setting than they can ever be in schools where going to the library is restricted to certain times or, worse, to a specific day of the week. This sort of arrangement is most unfortunate and can still be found in England as in America. It is unheard of in a junior school run along informal lines.

In junior schools, just as in some infant schools, many teachers try to provide a reading corner, where children can go to read in comfort and quiet. On occasion, we have seen children spend a whole day in a reading corner, enjoying an entire book with only an occasional interruption. These children are never exposed to readers or any reading text whatsoever. (Most of them would be astounded to know that sometimes whole classes of children are forced to read the same story at the same time in a reading lesson.)

This practice also allows for far greater variety in books. The head teacher can afford to buy a few copies of many different books, rather than one or two full sets of readers for an entire class. The children are exposed to all sorts of fiction, poetry, reference books, and other literature in this way.

As we mentioned in Chapter Three, junior schools face a major problem with their youngest children, who may have come from the infant school while in the midst of gaining confidence in their reading. The best solution, in the long run, may be to raise the age of leaving the infant school and to develop more effective means of communication between the infant and junior levels. At present, teachers are trying everything from formal reading programs—attempting to boost the child up—to informal approaches that give the child time to adjust to his new school. In the latter method, teachers recognize that a stimulating environment within the school is as important to the child's progress as additional help in areas where he is still weak.

We saw an example of this patience on the part of teachers in a school where many of the youngest children did some of their work in conjunction with the older nine-, ten-, and eleven-year-olds. There was initial concern, in the fall, that the youngest were not reading and writing enough and that they spent too much of their time working with the older children, observing superior writing and reading abilities without producing much on their own. Rather than assign these children to one type of reading or writing class, the decision was made to let them work as they were, with a great deal of support from their teachers. After two months of reticence on the part of the youngest junior group, many of them began to record their experiences spontaneously. They became involved in projects of deep importance to them, which led them to read on different subjects and induced them to write their feelings and impressions.

This approach reflects the careful thought being applied to the teaching of reading in many junior schools. It demonstrates the ability of the teachers to view learning as an experience that does not constantly include drill in such skills as reading and writing. The children's opportunity to observe and share in some of the work of their older classmates without being forced into any extended reading and writing of their own allowed them a period of growth without pressure and produced exciting results in the long run. When the children had branched out on projects that excited them, the teachers could help them with any specific reading problems that came up, in the context of other interests. They could thus approach their difficulties in a far less threatening way.

The kind of thinking applied to reading by some junior school teachers is sometimes extended to the teaching of mathematics, but less often. Just as in the United States, teachers are wary of modern mathematics and often unsure as to how it can best be taught. In the junior schools, it is the one subject that is almost invariably given a particular slot in each day's schedule, whereas other areas of the curriculum are dealt with more flexibly. We have spoken to mathematicians in colleges of education who contend that such scheduling is necessary. They argue that many teachers, because of their own backgrounds, remain most insecure with modern math. If they do not put it into the timetable, there is the danger it will be neglected for areas they find more enjoyable. In addition, some teachers feel — perhaps with justification — that many mathematical concepts can be learned only in isolation from other subjects.

In a substantial number of cases, junior-school teachers have treated modern math as a series of gimmicks to be larded on top of the traditional "basics." Some math books for children, designed to offer a very different approach, have been converted to texts and workbooks with which some children have to struggle just as they would with more traditional exercise books. This fate has befallen the very competent series of books *Lets Explore Mathematics,* by Leonard G. Marsh, which have become tattered exercise books in many schools rather than the innovative aids their author intended.[5] However, the picture of math teaching in junior schools is not completely bleak.

In many ways, the infant schools lead the junior schools in terms of work in mathematics. Many of the fine accomplishments in this area for juniors are derived from experiences the children have had in infant school. Children at the infant level learn the use of natural objects in some aspects of math. They also learn pictorial representation and some aspects of simple graphs. The junior schools are trying to build upon this knowledge, but it has taken them some time to develop the necessary materials.

Many teachers who experiment with modern math,

and go beyond the workbook, use the Nuffield Mathematics Project as the basis of their work. Nuffield math leaves a great deal to the discretion of the teacher, who must make the decisions about the kind of work that specific children need. The series, which now consists of twelve published pamphlets, is neither a syllabus nor a text for children. It proposes a way of looking at mathematics that teachers must try to understand before they can use it with children. It is a tribute to the Nuffield Project that so many junior teachers are examining its work and trying to use it.

A few junior schools engage in math that is innovative and derived from children's interests. Outdoor Math, as it is known to some American teachers, has a strong foothold in many junior schools. Children deal with large-scale and difficult measuring and mapping with interest and competence. For example, the work that goes into accurately establishing the area of an irregularly shaped field can be both detailed and complex. Ten- and eleven-year-olds sometimes work toward an understanding of algebra, largely through the complexities of graphing. Despite the difficulties for some teachers (who may have had no exposure to these new concepts of math, even in college), it is safe to say that a few are beginning to consider the potentials of exciting mathematical thinking. Many of the more inventive materials may help an unsure teacher to realize that mathematics can be enjoyable and challenging.

It must be emphasized that the work of high quality described throughout this chapter is produced without the competition of grades or the pressure of homework. Junior schools which work informally believe that neither grades nor homework is necessary. The talks the teacher has with the child about his work, the sight of a favorite story or drawing on the wall, are in themselves far more satisfying to the child than an imposed grade could ever be. These are things he cares about deeply, and the teacher recognizes his concern. Who can judge that Susan's poem is worth B-plus while John's story of foxes, not his best work, merits only a C-minus? If John is not doing as well as he might, his teacher will certainly talk to him about it—and probably find that the cause goes deeper than laziness or lack of interest.

One thing common to good junior classes is the freshness with which the children start the day. Work that is not completed on one occasion is begun the following day with interest. One reason for this is that school work stops when the school day ends. Many junior schools have no regular homework. When a particular topic is exciting to a child, he may take home a relevant book to read. Poems and stories are often written at home, not because one is due the next day, but simply because the writer wanted to write and knew the work would receive attention and interest in school.

Many teachers find this hard to believe. Surely only the "best" children would take the time to write a poem at home unless they were asked to. But much of what we have seen—in good English schools—indicates that things do not work out this way. Writing and other projects are done for the child's pleasure and that of his peers, as well as for his teacher. Many children come to school with unsolicited work of all sorts and it does not necessarily go straight to the teacher. We have seen short stories handed around among friends in a classroom long before the teacher knows they have been written.

It is true that some children will never produce certain kinds of work without being required to do so. This is something the good teacher can deal with best in school. He can urge them to do their writing, or reading, or math, and keep a close watch on their work. In his mind, it would be a major error to pressure them to write something after school under the guise of homework. There is so much of life for a child of primary age to explore after school hours that many teachers in England have no desire to ask the child to sit at a desk at home.

The paramount focus on getting into secondary school is fading steadily in districts that have abolished the eleven-plus exam. There is growing confidence in the integral worth of junior schools themselves. They want the children to enjoy life now. Many head teachers and others deeply involved in the schools feel that a child who is happy in school is better prepared and equipped to deal with the future.

A good junior school gives its children confidence to cope with a wealth of different situations. The students will be accustomed to variety, to choices, and to making decisions. Many will have substantial self-assurance, and they will know some areas of study that interest them. They will hope and expect that the work they encounter in secondary school will relate to their own lives and concerns. Only if they are very lucky will this last wish be fulfilled.

CHAPTER FIVE

The Whole Day Counts

THE LONG HALL of an infant school slowly fills with children. A class enters and sits on the floor, grouped around their teacher. She whispers something to them, and they begin to sing as the rest of the school files in. Children from other classes recognize the song and join in. The hall resounds. When the song ends, all the children are seated in a large circle on the floor. The head teacher stands near the door. For a long moment, teachers and children listen to the silence.

"Shall we sing the songs from our harvest festival?" asks the head. Each class in turn stands to sing one song about the harvest. It is not a performance; there is no accompaniment. The children huddle close to their teacher, who sings with them, helping them over a verse that is hard to remember. Each song touches upon a different aspect of the harvest. The children who are listening sway slowly to the rhythm of the music.

The last class to stand performs a choral reading that they composed with the guidance of their teacher, a skilled musician. The words describe the harvest from the planting of the seeds to the celebrations in the fall. Other members of the class accompany the speakers with music: poetic sounds composed by a group of children who play drums, a tambourine, a small xylophone, and other percussive instruments. The words "growing grain" rise above a low rustling sound. A staccato beat emphasizes the cutting of the wheat. The words and the music are inseparable and have a startling effect on the audience. The children lean forward to catch the sounds and watch as different instruments join in. The reading ends.

The head teacher smiles and thanks everyone for singing. The children file silently out of the hall, moving quickly and quietly. A few begin to hum a last song which they carry with them down the corridors to their classroom.

This assembly, held at midmorning in the fall, illustrates the feeling of community that pervades the best schools in England. The technical reason for this gathering is an anachronistic law which requires each school to start the day with a religious assembly. This infant school, like quite a few others, has found that there are many ways to interpret the word "religious." The assembly gives the head a chance to bring teachers and children together to share experiences. A group of children may tell the rest of the school about a special project they have been working on. Someone points out a new display of unusual rocks on a table nearby. A group holds up a series of drawings they have made, showing different varieties of birds. A girl stands to tell the school about the new baby guinea pigs recently born in her classroom. It is a time for discussion, for singing, for children and teachers to discover things about each other.

This unusual use of the assembly period illustrates an important aspect of life in outstanding schools. The teachers who call their school or classroom a "community" feel that a child's day in school should possess unity of purpose. Everything that happens to him in the course of a day is important to his growth and affects his work in the classroom. A number of schools in England act on this belief and are pleased with the results

Schools everywhere are concerned with the breaks during the day—recess, the lunch period, special gatherings. These breaks can cause both problems and pleasure in a school. At the same time, teachers welcome the minutes during the day when they may have the opportunity to sit down and relax with colleagues.

In England as in the United States, there are still schools which treat these breaks in classroom routine as times for teachers to escape children. Someone—a teacher, an aid—is left on duty in the playground or indoors while the door to the teachers' lounge hides the rest of the staff. This is a particular problem at lunchtime. Should the teachers be in the lunch room to supervise? Should they have the time free to do as they please? Or should they join in the meal, making it an important aspect of the day in school?

Some English schools deal with these questions in a number of intriguing ways. The midmorning and midafternoon breaks are fairly short. In the morning, there is free milk for those who want it, followed by fifteen to twenty minutes of time to play, outdoors if possible. Teachers everywhere recognize that these play periods are valuable. The change of environment is important, as is the chance to see students from other classes. Children gather in large numbers to play a game— dodge ball, soccer, or many others. They look forward to seeing friends, to the chance to talk, to race, or to play quietly.

These breaks, and the opportunity to be outside the

building, should not be an escape from the classroom. In a number of infant and junior schools, children move freely from room to room without question. They engage in many different kinds of work during the day, some of it involving the whole body, some of it quiet and relaxed. Going outside does not, therefore, mean a release from severe constraints. The explosion of energy that always occurs as children rush out onto the playground does not turn into violent or hectic and pointless activity. If it does, something is wrong inside the school. Someone does not allow the children to express themselves sufficiently during the rest of the day.

A group of teachers supervises morning and afternoon breaks of similar length. They give the rest of the staff a chance to relax and have a cup of coffee or tea in the staff room. Both breaks are important for the teachers. After ten or fifteen minutes they return to the classroom, ready to enjoy the rest of the morning or the afternoon and to work more effectively with the children.

An attractive alternative to these scheduled breaks is practiced in some schools which feel that the day should be as unified as the child's learning. They do not break the child's work into subjects, and they feel that his day should also avoid these artificial halts. Under this system, classes or groups of children go outside when they wish during the course of the day. This gives them more outdoor space when they need it and works particularly well when the classroom has direct access to the playground.

Schools that have adopted this practice feel it has many positive attributes. Teachers find that many children are deeply involved in a project in the middle of the morning. We have often heard children complain when the teacher announces that it is time for a break. Different children need varying amounts of time to work on a project. Some children want to continue on a piece of writing for the whole morning. Others need a quick run in the yard after an hour's work. A more flexible schedule makes allowance for differences. In addition, teachers do not like to discriminate between work time and play time, between the classroom and the playground. The activity a child engages in outside may be just as important as a project pursued at a writing table.

The only disadvantage of these unscheduled breaks is that it becomes more difficult to arrange a time for the teachers to meet together. There are two solutions to this problem. In some infant and junior schools, relationships between children and teachers are such that a teacher feels he can leave his class for five or ten minutes at midmorning for coffee. Not all teachers go at the same time. In other schools, a teacher may go to the staff room, get a cup of coffee, and come back to the class. The loss of time to converse in the staff room is offset in these schools by casual contacts between teachers—a few words in the hall, cooperative teaching of some kind, or a visit to another room to borrow materials or share an idea. In any case, the long break after lunch still exists.

The day in an infant and junior school is longer than is common in the United States, but the children do not spend the additional time in the classrooms. School starts about nine o'clock, ends at a quarter to four or four o'clock, and includes an hour and a half for lunch and free time. Lunch is an important occasion in many schools. One-half to two-thirds of the children usually remain for a hot dinner. Teachers and children gather— in a very different setting from the classroom—to share the meal and the conversation that goes with it.

There are many methods of organizing dining according to the size of the school and the design of the building. A large school often requires two sittings. In infant schools, where the tables seat eight or ten children, a teacher normally sits at every other table and serves much of the meal. The child decides what he wants and how much he can eat. In a few infant schools, serving dishes are passed around the tables so the children can serve themselves. Head teachers advocating this system have said to us, "Who are we to decide in any way how much the child should eat?"

In the junior schools, and in schools where juniors and infants eat together, a similar arrangement is made. The children bring trays from the kitchen to a server (a child or a teacher) who asks those at the table what they want before serving the food. "Dinner ladies," provided by the local education authority, come into the school for lunch. They help to prepare the meal and work in the dining room, clearing tables and dealing with any problems that may arise.

The organization of dining is important only as it is geared to making the meal a pleasant experience for all. This is no easy task. The effort fails in a number of schools, but it is made all over England in the belief that the meal is *not* an ordeal to sit through, but an essential part of the day. This attitude was well illustrated in a school where we ate on a few occasions.

In this school, infants and juniors eat together. The older students sit at the head of tables of about eight people; they bring in the food and serve it. Two children from the junior department are assigned to each table on a rotating basis to deal with these routines, and they generally consider it a privilege. Other children come to the tables as they wish and are not assigned anywhere. The teachers, the head teacher, people from the local education authority, or visitors in the building join tables at will. The food comes from the kitchen into the hall, the well-lit room that is also used as a gymnasium and meetingplace.

The child serving the food asks each person what he wants and provides it for him. There is usually meat, potatoes, and a vegetable, as well as substantial dessert. Occasionally there is salad. If a child does not want something, he is not forced to take it. Since the school would not want to pressure him into eating, it would be a waste to put unwanted food on his plate. He must eat what he asks for, unless he is sick. The same treatment is accorded teachers and all others.

A pleasant room and a friendly method of serving can provide the background for an enjoyable occasion. Teachers try to draw children into conversation. It is a chance to talk about things that do not come up in the classroom. There are many things that the children want to talk about among themselves. Since the schools attempt to deal with the children's own concerns and interests, children are likely to know quite a bit about each other and are able to talk freely. In addition, much of the work done in school is likely to excite curiosity — something that is on display across the room or seen through the door of another class may provoke discussion.

The teachers who eat with these children would never attempt to enforce silence. They encourage this kind of talk and would probably agree with John Dewey, who wrote:

> Enforced quiet and acquiescence prevent pupils from disclosing their real natures. They enforce artificial uniformity. They put seeming before being. They place a premium upon preserving the outward appearance of attention, decorum and obedience.[1]

These teachers spend much of the day encouraging the child to reveal his true nature in everything he does.

To enforce silence would negate that attempt. Because the teacher is involved in the discussion, because the children and the teacher know each other well, and because of the relaxed atmosphere in the room, the talk is animated and enjoyable for all.

To facilitate conversation, the noise level in a large dining area has to be fairly low. A number of schools accomplish this in two ways. First, there are no more than eight to ten pupils at a table. The tables are often round, focusing attention inward on the group. Second, the room is decently sound-proofed, with built-in panels and curtains. It is impossible to achieve a quiet dining room for children—or any other age level—without adequate sound proofing. We have seen schools which practice family dining (the term often used when small groups of children, of mixed ages, eat together), but lose its benefits because of a dining hall that magnifies every sound.

The children in England who stay at school for lunch generally eat meals that are well-cooked and varied. Parents pay the equivalent of twenty-one cents a day for the lunch and children either eat what is provided or else go home. They do not bring cold lunches to school. The additional expenses of the meals—which are substantial—are borne by the Department of Education and Science, a branch of the central government. Most large schools and new schools have their own kitchens, but older buildings often require deliveries from central kitchens serving ten or more schools. The hot meal system began during the Second World War because so many children were not getting balanced diets at home. It has continued for many reasons—one of them the recognition of the social value of the meal—but it has not lost its initial focus of a good meal for all who want it.

If a family does not have enough income to pay for a child's lunch, the school provides the money. The head teacher must interview the parents to establish a need, but teachers make an effort not to make the matter embarrassing to the child in the classroom. Of course, all the children eat the same meal at the same time regardless of who pays.

English teachers who enjoy their meals with the children are not paid an additional sum to come to lunch. Their meal is free. Teaching contracts stipulate that they cannot be required to eat with the children, but in many schools all the teachers do so, and in most at least a few join the students. They do not have to return directly to the classroom, because the mid-day break runs from noon to one thirty. The time after lunch is free for the children to play outside. Dinner ladies supervise them, while teachers have the time off.

The children leave the dining room one table at a time, as they finish their meal. While most go outside, some return to their classes with the teacher's permission, to continue some work too interesting to leave.

During the time from the end of lunch to the start of the afternoon session, children and teachers can be found throughout the building and outdoors. Some teachers prepare material in their classrooms instead of joining others in the staff room. Some are outside with the children. But none of this is unusual. In schools in many countries, and certainly in America, this is the common pattern of organization for the period immediately after lunch. What is worth noting here is the general attitude of the teachers to the children.

In keeping with the common feeling that the whole day is important to the child, many teachers do not seem to think of themselves as being either on or off duty. Of course, they enjoy a cup of tea with friends in the staff room, but if a child comes in with a problem or a request, he is generally answered and helped then — not forty-five minutes later when the school reopens. A small gesture, such as telling a child he can go ahead with some work in the classroom, or read in the library, and perhaps going with him to help in the search for a book, is very important. It encourages the child to feel that the teacher is there to aid him at any time and that the school is open to him as a resource throughout the day. These feelings are invaluable in giving the child a positive, comfortable attitude toward his school.

CHAPTER SIX

Freedom to Teach

THE BEST SCHOOLS in England are those which allow every member of the staff to make an important contribution to education. Teachers in England, whether in outstanding schools or in poor schools, enjoy a degree of freedom unknown in many parts of the world. When this freedom is accompanied by a feeling of trust among staff members, and a positive belief in the capabilities of each teacher, the result is often superior education for the children. While it is not easy to achieve this type of setting, we have been deeply impressed by the number of schools whose staffs do work together, as teams, for the mutual benefit of children and teachers.

The most influential and decisive individual in this system is the man or woman who runs the school. In English primary schools, the head is, above all else, an experienced and knowledgeable teacher. He is not promoted *out* of the ranks of teachers, but is elevated to the most responsible position a teacher can hold. The title "head teacher" is very consciously applied to the leader of the school.

The presence of a good head teacher is felt throughout the school. A substantial number of heads spend the greater part of their days in the classrooms, working directly with the children and their teachers.

Unlike American principals or head teachers in traditional English schools, the head of a school run along informal lines enjoys a position of relaxed authority. If the school is run well, the children develop a sense of responsibility and self-control, which alleviates the head's role as supreme disciplinarian. He is then an educator, not just an administrator. His entry into the classroom is a natural occurrence and will hardly be noticed if the children are deeply involved in their work. They think of him as another adult who can give advice or help with a problem. It is not the least bit unusual for a child to ask the head teacher how to spell a word, to tell him about a recent experience, show him a piece of finished work, or simply sit down with him for a chat.

In the same way, the teacher who has known the head for a time is not threatened by his presence; he is glad to see him. The good teacher relishes the chance to talk to another adult or to ask advice about a particular aspect of the work in progress.

Needless to say, this is not the norm in all schools. There are schools in England where the head still prefers the more autocratic title of "headmaster" or "headmistress." He or she will feel far more comfortable seated in the sanctuary of an office that is inaccessible to children and teachers. Many local authorities make a conscious effort to keep head teachers from slipping into the role of an administrator and disciplinarian distant from staff and children. Educators caution the head teacher to live up to the full meaning of his title; to see his function in terms of teaching and educational leadership, not administration.[1]

When the head teacher and the staff gather in a school's staff room, they constitute the group that makes many decisions about that particular school. A primary school in England has substantial leeway in decision making and is not rigidly controlled by higher authority. The head teacher and the staff decide on the materials and equipment they want in the building, based upon a known budget. They plan the curriculum, there being no fixed curricula for any group of schools. Even the hiring of new staff is largely the responsibility of the head teacher in each school.

There are, however, a number of controls on the freedom of each head teacher. Primary schools are technically governed by boards of managers, who officially approve appointments, renovations to the building, and certain other items.[2] At first glance, they seem to compare with local school boards in the United States, but in fact they have very little power. Theirs is residual authority, which had substantial influence over the affairs of local schools in the nineteenth century, but which has largely given way to the local education authority, or L.E.A. The L.E.A. functions within the framework of the County Council or, in cities, the Borough Council. The director of the L.E.A. is generally known as the Chief Education Officer and is appointed by the education committee of the Council.

Although head teachers view their Chief Education Officer as superior to them in the hierarchy, his role differs from the position of a Superintendent of Schools in America. The Chief Education Officer provides a great deal of help to the schools in his area. His office centralizes purchasing for commonly needed supplies. He has substantial voice in the selection of head teachers, and through his staff, he is responsible for school construction and maintenance. In addition, he must handle the local education authority's relationship with the central government's Department of Education and Science in London. He and his staff have an important role in communication and the exchange of ideas among teachers within their area (an aspect of their work discussed more fully in Chapter Seven).

Within his district, the Chief Education Officer may be the guardian of each school's independence, or he may exercise substantial negative influence. Some Chief Education Officers put heavy pressure on inferior head teachers until they improve their schools or resign. Some deny sufficient money for books but buy expensive equipment that teachers do not want. Still, the head teacher retains remarkable freedom in most situations. This independence is not a guarantee of better schooling or improved relationships among staff members, it is simply an encouragement.

While a great deal of responsibility and paperwork accompany the independence enjoyed by English head teachers, they do not suffer from the same burden of forms and reports that we have seen in large American school systems. In small schools in England, containing three or four classrooms, the head teacher often has a class of his own. In all larger schools he is in a position to choose between teaching or coping with administrative details. One of the finest heads we met acknowledged, "I often let the paperwork go. My job is working with the children and I get to the other when I can."

If the school is of substantial size (more than six classes), the head usually has a secretary to help with paperwork. Except in the very smallest schools, there is also a deputy head, a teacher who normally has a class of his own, but is prepared to take on extra responsibilities that the head teacher delegates to him. The deputy receives a higher salary than the other teachers and often works closely with the head on many of the school's affairs.

The position of deputy headship offers a talented teacher the chance to work toward a higher post, to learn from the extra responsibility while still doing what he is best at—teaching children. Teachers who are new to the school may learn a great deal about the school's educational aims by watching the deputy at work in the classroom.

When difficulties arise between members of the staff and the head teacher (as they naturally do even in the best schools), the deputy can usually help out. Because he has a class of his own and is directly involved with the children, teachers are less likely to regard him as a threatening figure. In many cases the deputy can help to keep channels of communication open between members of the staff. Hostility among teachers inhibits the sharing of ideas and information, an exchange which is essential to the success of informal methods in a school.

An atmosphere of cooperation allows the staff to develop their own approaches to teaching within the building, adapting methods to the children. An example of this is found in a Leicestershire infant school.

The flexible, "open" plan of the school allows teachers and children to move freely from one space to another.[3] Classrooms are only partially enclosed, their fourth side opening into central areas which children of all classes can use together for different purposes. At the same time, there are places of retreat where a group of children or a whole class unit can work privately and quietly on its own. The school runs in an effective and informal manner. The children, while using the many areas available to them, remain under the supervision of one teacher for the whole day.

When we visited this school, the head teacher and her deputy were working closely with the staff to expand the use of the building and to take advantage of the talents of individual teachers. They wanted to give children the chance to move from one member of the staff to another for different projects, while returning to their own class unit at least three times during each day.

Teachers who have worked this way in other schools are sometimes skeptical about its worth with very young children. For this reason, the head teacher and staff at this school moved slowly, with cautious consideration and with visits to other infant schools that were successful in this method. Their own school, already an exceptional environment for five- to seven-year-olds, would not take steps to reorganize for at least a year. But what is of greatest importance here is to note the way the staff approached these revisions.

Although the ideas originated with the head and the deputy, they are now the property of the whole group. Discussions involving every member of the staff grew out of a general recognition that reorganization of the day and patterns of teaching could not work without unanimity of feeling. Because the head teacher and the deputy approached the staff as equals, the plan became a joint one. Everyone was concerned with the implications of change.

In a small school such as this one (six classes) debate and involvement is possible. In the long run, it seems likely that the experience will prove valuable to the teachers, even if they decide to keep the children grouped in class units. Yet it does not always fall to the head teacher to put forth major ideas and start discussion. Some heads are particularly concerned that their teachers' ideas find support.

In one infant school in London, a head teacher told us of the origins of recent changes. We found her in an ancient building, situated in a poor neighborhood. Teaching there had been so unrewarding under the previous head that few children had had the same teacher for a full school year. While this had terrible effects on the students and on the morale of the school, it did mean that the new head teacher was able to recruit a new staff, largely of her own choosing. These teachers were eager to do away with the rigid classroom structure that gripped the school, but they were unsure about the head's position. Four teachers joined together and worked out a plan to combine their classes and their skills. They outlined the need for major changes in the building, including the removal of some walls, the installation of movable partitions, and the addition of covered, outdoor play spaces. The group drew up their plan in detail and went to the head, confident that she would listen but afraid that she might reject their ideas. Instead, her response was "Let's get on with it!"

The head told us later that she was delighted with the way this had happened. The teachers had presented her with a scheme that was similar to the goals she had in mind for the school. But she had been afraid to move too fast and impose her ideas on a staff not yet ready to change. Now, because the ideas originated with the teachers, she was prepared to help with her own talents and to try to get the financial support needed for alterations to the building. These teachers, who were shortly able to put their plan into action, circumvented one of the major obstacles to team teaching by agreeing among themselves to work as a group and to share classes. There was no outside direction involved in their early planning and they were a committed team before they had the facilities to operate as one.

Both the head teacher and her staff have an enormous stake in this school. They are now partners in an enterprise which succeeds because they believe in it. The head works with her staff, not above them. She is like the head teacher of another school who described his staff as, "my colleagues." In his case, as in others in England, this is an honest expression of equality which leads to better teaching. Unfortunately, such equality is still lacking in many English schools.

As in some areas of England, the American teacher who wants to effect change often beats his head against an unyielding wall. His only freedoms may be negative. He can, for example, "lock the door" of his classroom, as Herbert Kohl describes in *36 Children*. He then works alone, shuts out the rest of the school, and suffers the constant disapproval of teachers and administrators more concerned with classroom efficiency than the needs of children. He may choose to work against or around the existing curriculum, again a reaction against a policy of some kind rather than a fresh start with a positive plan.

A major difference between American and English primary education lies in the democratic character of an increasing number of English schools, compared with the alarmingly autocratic atmosphere that often reigns in the United States. The head of a good English school often believes that his teachers will find their own successful ways to work with children, including the establishment of individual programs and schedules. The head expects that each teacher will contribute positively to the life of the school.

This is not to laud every English head teacher. The majority of English primary schools are not run informally and a large portion of head teachers maintain an autocratic image. Many indulge in outright commands. Others speak of everything that happens in the school in the first person singular: "I like bright colors and art on the walls, as you can see from the work of these children." But statements such as this, made in front of the children who did the paintings and the class teacher who encouraged their work, are becoming more and more of a rarity. Martinet head teachers have disappeared in some areas, allowing men and women willing to share the decisions of the school with the whole staff to take their place.

Schools which take a less formal approach to teaching and learning place many difficult demands on the staff. In running an informal class, the individual teacher takes on more responsibility than he would assume in a traditional class. He is usually responsible for a large portion of the curriculum. He must develop many different programs, providing a stimulating environment that allows him both to lead and to follow the children's interests.

One of the most extraordinary aspects of English education is the large number of talented teachers who are working imaginatively with children despite their previous training. The institutions which train teachers are, on the whole, a bleak and depressing feature of English higher education. A sad example is the finding of a national survey which showed that "77.9 per cent of students at colleges of education considered their professional training inadequate."[4] Few teachers or observers of English schools offer any reason for success in teaching among so many who were poorly prepared for their profession.

The men and women who come to work in state primary schools have generally undertaken a different pattern of training than that followed by American teachers. Upon graduating from a secondary school, most students who want to teach go to a college of education, where a three-year course leads to qualification—which is a certificate to teach—but not a degree. A few go to a university and take courses toward a B.A. degree. A third alternative, only recently available, is to study for a Bachelor of Education degree, a four-year program in a college of education. But the basic difference in training to teach in England as compared to the United States is the time in the student's life at which the first decisions have to be made.

A secondary student in England with an interest in teaching must commit himself to attending a college of education sometime during his seventeenth year. If he has an opportunity to go on to a university, he must accept or reject this chance at seventeen, for only about 5 per cent of students completing secondary school in England are offered university places.

If a student chooses a teaching career and enters a college of education, as over 90 per cent of those now teaching have done, he will join an institution where virtually all the faculty are ex-schoolteachers. Many colleges of education have been biased against hiring scholars with no professional teaching experience at the primary or secondary level. In addition, the best of such scholars are lured to the universities by prestige, if nothing else. One result is that the breadth of instruction in the liberal arts and other fields that the student needs often suffers from constant return to issues of the classroom and children on the part of the faculty. The argument is sometimes posed that the student received the general background he needed in secondary school; occasionally this is true. But it fails to account for the different tastes and levels of understanding shown by a sixteen-year-old in secondary school and the same individual at nineteen in a college of education.

The student himself is likely to be of high caliber. Since so few secondary school graduates are admitted to the universities, some very fine students enroll in colleges of education. If the universities draw upon approximately the top 5 per cent, the colleges of education are able to select their students from the next 5 or at most 10 per cent of those who complete secondary school.

Yet in most instances the training of these future teachers remains a dull and formal affair. Many students sit and listen passively as the knowledge they may or may not need is expounded to them. Despite the tutorial system, which brings the student into close contact with some members of the faculty, many training colleges fail to encourage personal relationships between faculty and students and ignore the varied interests of the students in creating their curriculum. Yet, this is exactly what the colleges urge the new teachers to accomplish in their classrooms when they finish their training.

There are wonderful exceptions to this situation. In a few colleges of education, students are involved in courses that allow them to explore and develop their own creativity in painting, crafts, and prose. What they learn in this way should allow them to better help the children, while it also expands their own horizons. At one college we visited, an impressive course gave students an idea of how to cope with teaching reading. In addition to competent lectures and discussions, students went to nearby schools repeatedly for diagnostic and remedial work with children of different ages. The visits to the schools interlocked week by week with the course work at the college and allowed students to discuss the teaching of reading on the basis of immediate practical experience. Regrettably, such intelligent instruction is rare and complaints about training remain widespread. Head teachers are the most vocal and complain first about the number of students pressed upon them for practice teaching; at the same time, they claim that their new teachers have not had sufficient practical experience.

Among teachers we have talked to who were trained in the last ten years, very few praise the experience. Their criticisms are twofold. Some speak of a limited breadth of background and say they were not introduced to enough fine literature or to a specialized subject, particularly in the sciences, that might help them later. Many more teachers are critical of their training to teach specific subjects, with mathematics, reading, and science mentioned most often.

The training colleges in England have many improvements to make in the experiences they offer prospective teachers. At the same time, English teacher education does not fall below that in the United States. Robert Fisher, an American professor teaching temporarily at an English college of education, comments:

> The two systems of teacher education are hardly comparable. An American professor cannot help but be favorably impressed by an English college of education when compared with the mass production methods at American colleges and universities, by the low staff-student ratio, [and] the importance of small tutorial sessions. . . . Provisions for teaching practice are far superior to those offered American students.[5]

Those few teachers who enter the profession as university graduates have had a wholly different experience. They have majored in any one of a variety of subjects, but almost never in education per se. Their liberal arts background has been generally better (although more specialized), and their teachers more qualified, than at the colleges of education. Although most university graduates who have turned to teaching have gone into secondary schools, more now consider primary education as a field that offers greater opportunities, even though the pay is less. Beginning in 1970, university students who lacked education courses had to take one year of postgraduate studies before becoming qualified.

An encouraging trend in England is the large numbers of male students who decide to teach in primary schools. For some years, only a few men taught in the junior schools; in 1955, most head teachers at the junior level were women. Today a majority are men. As yet, only a few men have chosen to teach in infant schools, but those who do may lure others toward work with this age group. The English primary schools are thus successful in destroying the old adage that only women are suitable for work with young children.

When new teachers complete their studies, observations, and teaching practices, and have full-time jobs, they have yet to become part of their new school. Their acclimatization to the job is particularly important in schools working in informal ways. These teachers do not receive system-wide curriculum guides or text books to form the core of a subject. In their first months in school they will need a lot of help and advice, yet not to the point of having the head teacher or anyone else dictate how their classes should develop.

The job of aiding the new teacher falls mainly to the head of the school. We have seen many approaches to the initiation of a new staff member, each dependent on the individuals and the kinds of work going on in the building. The teacher must have a great deal of positive support, but not too much direction or invasion of the classroom. Leonard Marsh, creator of the *Let's Explore Mathematics* series, observes:

The problem for the young teacher is to become sensitive to the varying work rhythms of individual children and, in the first instance, to know how to slow down the class pattern in order to obtain control of the work situation.[6]

While the best head teachers are often those with strong convictions about teaching, most would agree that it is vital for the new teacher to find his own way with the children. Much as a head might be tempted to direct a new teacher, the sensitive man or woman will stand back and spend the first few weeks of a term watching. The head may do his best to observe the strengths and weaknesses of the new teacher and enter the classroom to help, rather than to instruct. This attitude mirrors the school's work with the children. A teacher spends a large amount of time watching the children and then tries to provide an atmosphere that will draw out their interests. In the same way, the good head teacher is determined to respect the personality and concerns of the new teacher and to offer help and support where needed. A new teacher, given this sort of treatment, is more likely to feel that his ideas and concerns are important to the school. This, in turn, encourages classroom teaching of fine quality. This type of experience also suggests that a remarkable number of schools in England have fostered excellence in teaching—despite the colleges of education.

The classrooms of good schools reflect the talents of each teacher. The sensitive head is proud to point out the staff member who is skilled in art or music, or who has a special interest in drama. One classroom that we visited had been turned into Sherwood Forest by the children. Trees, leaves, and animals were everywhere—hanging from the ceiling, painted on the windows. The walls were covered with the children's work on forestry, Robin Hood, the costumes of the period, and descriptions of life in the forest. The children initiated the idea. They wanted to have Sherwood Forest in the classroom. Thanks to their teacher's artistic talent, they transformed the room into a fantasy of greens and browns. Their interests and hers meshed to produce work of excellent quality.

In schools which trust both teacher and child, no two classes could be alike. There is always the opportunity for individual ideas and personalities to emerge and for less skilled teachers to grow. One of the best ways to understand how this process is encouraged is to visit the staff room of a particularly fine primary school. It is here that teachers gather in free time during the day. There is always coffee or tea available, in rooms that are comfortably furnished and provide a place to relax and talk.

These gatherings are essential to the life of the school. They give the teachers a break from their strenuous and demanding work with the children. A school operating in a flexible, creative manner must have such meetings frequently. They allow for a daily exchange of ideas and information on an informal basis and foster feelings of friendship and cooperation between teachers whose good work is the key to each child's success.

The conversation in a staff room may run in any direction, but the exciting aspect of it is that so much of the talk is about children, the school, and the issues that concern it. In most primary schools, the head teacher will join these meetings, and he or she often raises questions or problems that can be dealt with in casual conversation. The example of one staff room will give an indication of the kinds of gatherings that occur in a number of schools.

The room is at the end of a wing of a modern building. It is comfortably furnished, with a number of armchairs; and against one wall is a long counter with coffeepots and teapots and cupboard space beneath it. When the staff gathers in this room, the head teacher will join them, for this is the room from which the school is really run. The head believes it is part of his job to be there with the staff. Amid jokes and the relaxed aura of the room, decisions and plans are made every day. People drift in and out at the breaks, depending on the amount of time they want to take away from their classrooms.

Important discussions of the curriculum take place there, both to help a teacher with an immediate problem of the day and to plan long-term aims. Ideas are broached to see what the general reaction may be: a week-long study trip with thirty ten- and eleven-year-olds to a rural nature center, or a plan for retired grandparents to sign up to drive small groups of children short distances to museums or other places of immediate interest.

Not all the staff is present for these discussions, but as ideas are shared over a period of days, general reactions become clear. Decision making is less formal and responses perhaps more candid than they would be in a scheduled staff meeting. The head values these gatherings for many reasons. He keeps in touch with his staff personally and professionally. He is able to offer his services on the spot to make arrangements, follow up on problems, and generally try to take over some of the burden of the classroom teacher's work.

It is in the staff room as well as in the classroom that the most valuable aspects of English primary education are found. In these rooms, the moment by moment decisions are made that affect the operation of the school. A healthy, trusting, and cheerful environment in a staff room will often have a major effect on classrooms and on the children themselves.

CHAPTER SEVEN

Partners in Innovation

CLASSROOM TEACHERS HAVE long had a great deal to say about educational innovation in England. Experienced and talented teachers dominate the membership of most innovative bodies and keep ideas flowing out from the schools and then back into the classroom. G. W. Bassett sums up the immense importance of this practice, writing:

> . . . it should be recognized that to strengthen the professional freedom of the teacher is the surest way to guarantee a continuing concern for progressive ideas, and that all steps taken to introduce or accelerate change should promote, or at least be in accord with, this professional freedom.[1]

One of the prime aims of agencies concerned with educational innovation in England is to encourage greater cooperation among teachers and, in this way, to draw upon the talents of individuals at every level of the system. Cooperation is by no means the norm throughout the primary schools; indeed some English teachers still feel that their independence is best maintained when the door of their classroom is closed to the outside world. This feeling has existed in America and Great Britain for years. The teacher has long regarded his classroom as a sanctuary where he works on his own with forty children. A teacher who works in such isolation might read about new developments outside the school, yet remain ignorant of a talented colleague at work next door.

Gradually, educators in both countries have attempted to change this attitude, often with success. They realize that there is much to gain from cooperation between staff members and that isolated teaching can have a negative and debilitating effect on all sorts of teachers, from the best to the weakest. Those who try to be innovative need support and reassurance; those who are unable to cope need to watch others at work and to learn how to use positive advice from the outside. The innovative agencies in England thus have two very closely connected aims: first, to spread ideas which originate, for the most part, in the schools; and second, to open the classroom doors and get teachers to talk and work together.

During the last ten to twenty years in England, teachers have become more open to the idea of working cooperatively within schools and have also participated readily in the spread of ideas from one area to another. A teacher who is willing to accept ideas from outside the classroom, and who feels he has something to give in return, may first find that he is helped most by another member of the staff in his own building. If the local education authority is an open one, which provides for good communication between schools, this teacher may also discover that the L.E.A.'s services are essential to teaching of high quality. If he is talented, he may have the chance to contribute to the dissemination of his own ideas throughout the local authority.

Because the services of the local education authority can have a profound influence on individual schools, we will consider their work before moving to a discussion of innovation on a national level. There are a number of ways in which the L.E.A. can make its presence felt in the schools. By far the most impressive and effective method is through an advisory service directed toward all the schools in the area.

ADVISERS

A number of advisory services have made a vital contribution to the remarkable primary school education available for children in many parts of England. Their many activities provide forms of communication and advice otherwise unknown in schools, in England and elsewhere. Wherever they operate, the advisory services are staffed by experienced teachers and specialists who can make direct contributions to schools by aiding teachers in the classroom. They diagnose problems, help with staff difficulties, improve communication between schools, and provide in-service education throughout the authority.

An adviser can be found far from his office, working directly with children in a great variety of settings. He shares his talents and knowledge with the group and observes the relationships that are at work among children and their teacher. His colleagues, sometimes numbering up to twenty in one county, may work with many different educational services. One organizes a meeting to improve communications between junior-school teachers and their secondary-school colleagues. Another, seated at a table with a group of interested eleven-year-olds, poses practical problems to introduce geometric progressions. Elsewhere, an adviser takes a small group out of a class to test their reading ability and find ways of helping the teacher deal with their difficulties. Meetings with the central authority keep each adviser informed on events in the county.

In good authorities, the adviser feels that an essential part of his job is to provide teachers with positive help. However, advisory services were not always geared toward aiding teachers, nor were they as approachable as they are today. They originated in local inspectorates and were founded by some local education authorities to keep even closer tabs on their schools than the Her Majesty's Inspectorate of Schools[2] could do. A number of L.E.A.s still title these individuals "local inspectors," and in a few areas they devote more time to this role than to constructive advice and counsel. Many L.E.A.s have no such body at all; in other areas, advisers exist but are so understaffed that they cannot reach all the schools effectively. Within a few authorities the advisers are pressed into administrative tasks and lose both their independence and the time to perform their primary functions. But these are problems within advisory systems that can be rectified.

We looked most closely at advisory work in the city of Bristol and in the counties of Oxfordshire, Leicestershire, and the West Riding of Yorkshire, although these are certainly not the only local education authorities where good advisory work takes place.[3] While no two authorities establish advisory programs in the same way, some common patterns exist.

The success of an advisory system is determined to a large extent by the personality and direction of the Chief Education Officer, whose leadership naturally affects the quality of education throughout the authority. While individual schools have always been able to exert strong leadership in an area, the Chief

Education Officer is often largely responsible for change on a county-wide basis. His position is of utmost importance. Where he is talented and progressive, schools are likely to respond with positive education for their children.

But the Chief Education Officer cannot accomplish change on his own. A good advisory staff plays an important role in the communication of new ideas to schools. Because the advisory staff is dependent upon their Chief Education Officer for salary and promotion, much of its work must reflect his philosophy and goals. Yet the best officers, in charge of progressive areas, permit staff members to use their own discretion often and encourage them to feel that they are not always bound by official opinion. Advisory work is most successful where a delicate relationship is maintained that gives advisers some degree of independence, while allowing the Chief Education Officer to formulate and act upon general policy.

Advisers are most effective when they enter the schools in an unthreatening way. In one authority, the Chief Education Officer has gone so far as to say that his advisers will have no say in the promotion of teachers. His aim is to impress teachers that they can approach advisers on any matter of concern without fear that what they say will come back to haunt their careers at a later date. If teachers feel comfortable enough to admit mistakes, and to talk with the adviser as an equal, the system is functioning well.

When an adviser enters a school he usually looks for the head teacher. Often he can be of more help to the head than he can to the other members of the staff—not only because of the head teacher's decision-making position, but also because of the loneliness of the job. Despite good staff relationships, the head teacher, like the American principal, has many things to mull over alone.

In addition, the head teacher does not always have much time to visit other schools (although some authorities make provision for it). The adviser can fill him in on different activities in the authority. The head welcomes this chance to share problems with the advisor, a man or woman who knows the school, but who can stand back and listen with an impartial ear. The head will be reassured to know that other schools face problems similar to his own, and that the advisor backs his decisions and is willing to spend time helping him over any major difficulties.

The discussion of school affairs and the time spent in classes leave the adviser well informed and better able to help or to exchange ideas in the next school he visits. With their range of special abilities, advisers bring practical and valuable aid to many teachers. The adviser must, however, gain entrance to the classroom on a friendly and casual basis. He must come in as the teacher's equal and without any pretense of superior authority.

Advisers sometimes steer away from schools where they have not been invited by a head or classroom teacher. Although this may restrict their work, it keeps them free of the image of inspectors. The boundaries of their county or city are small enough so that they can know head teachers and many classroom teachers throughout the area. An adviser can enter a school comfortably, with the knowledge that he or she can best help and share positive ideas by working alongside the teacher, with the children.

The relationship of adviser to teacher depends upon the teacher's understanding that the adviser is not there to judge or report, but to help. This works in a number of situations that we have observed, but it is very difficult to achieve. Teachers in England are as sensitive of their prerogatives as are teachers in America, although in fact English teachers often do have more independence than their counterparts in the United States. Advisers, however, always run the risk of telling a teacher how to do something, rather than convincing him that a different method might improve his class's work. This complicates the adviser's role and tends to encourage the growth of specialist advisers, who introduce wholly new work into the schools, offending few teachers in the bargain.

The specialists work in many fields. Advisers competent to give teachers help in tie dying, fabric printing, pottery, woodwork, and art of all sorts are very popular. Some advisory services put great emphasis on music. They try to provide access to a variety of instruments and give teachers the confidence to work with children in this area. Advisers also give help in drama, reading, language development, and movement.

In the more traditional subject areas, specialists in math are fairly common—and are desperately needed in some schools. Science advisers, however, seldom appear in primary schools. Some L.E.A.s—although highly successful with programs in art—have failed to give teachers the boost that is needed to help them understand newer methods in science.

Despite their talents in various fields, advisers are not always successful in reaching teachers. Many advisers have to guard against the common criticism that they tend to go only where they are welcome and never to schools where their relations with the staff are not good. Even in good authorities, advisers are guilty of neglecting such schools, which need help the most. A school suffers if cut off from a number of advisers. It may become part of an out-group within the

L.E.A., seldom visited and little-known in comparison with its more popular neighbors. Any talented teachers in these schools may feel tempted to leave the authority when they realize that the advisers are unaware of their work.

Counties in which advisory services are active often provide extensive in-service education for teachers to counteract some of this criticism. They do this in conjunction with a number of other bodies, depending on the area and the subject matter. We consider in-service education in the next section of this chapter, but it is important to note that in taking a large interest in this work, the adviser can keep in touch with teachers in whose rooms he may not be welcome. The in-service courses also allow advisers to share, on a wide scale, ideas and practices that have been developed in the schools of the area. From what we have seen, this is very attractive to teachers. They are more impressed with ideas and materials shown at an in-service course if they have been used with success in nearby schools.

The advisory services which we have seen in active operation are immensely important to the success of the schools in their region. They provide services that could be dispensed in no other way. Most importantly, they form a steady but informal link between the schools, which allows for a level of communication between teachers and head teachers that is unknown in areas where such a service does not exist. It is fair to say that counties that are famous for large numbers of innovative schools are counties that have active and strong advisory services.

IN-SERVICE EDUCATION AND TEACHERS' CENTERS

In-service education is essential for primary-school teachers all over England. The Plowden Report was outspoken about this:

> The unique freedom of the English schools is defensible only
> if teachers prove themselves equipped to meet demands which
> are increasingly exacting. The three-year course is no more
> than a basis. In-service training provides a necessary super-
> structure.[4]

Some local education authorities have begun to provide
in-service education in teachers' centers scattered
through their areas and in larger, residential centers
owned by a few authorities. There has been substantial
encouragement for both types of centers. The Plowden
Report argues particularly for the local centers, where
"equipment and materials can be tried out and discussed and the ideas gained at residential courses can
be appraised after being tested in the schools."[5]

Available to teachers throughout the country, the
in-service courses range from very specific scientific
and mathematical subjects to experimental art. The
best are with indirect reference to the classroom. Many
residential courses allow the teacher to sample and
choose the subjects he wants to work with after his arrival. Other residential courses are geared toward in-
depth exploration of one subject. A weekend course
in music could involve a variety of activities, from
listening to and discussing sonatas to singing or making percussive instruments.

The men and women who run many of the residential
courses strive to deal with the whole individual during
the course of the weekend or the week, just as they
hope the teacher will do with his children. In addition
to work which may become part of school curricula,
many of the sessions try to provide an experience at
the teacher's level in the subject matter at hand and
then a discussion of the kinds of work children might
do in the same field. Teachers need to understand the
process of learning in many different areas, and they

do this best if they come to different concepts on their own, not at a childish, level.

The residential centers offer some cultural experience as part of the course—the chance to listen to music, or view a film, or hear a reading of poetry. This may be followed by discussion. There is also an effort to provide a variety of possibilities for informal recreation. The teachers at these sessions should leave with more to think about and remember than simply a new approach to some subject matter in school. There is thus a substantial effort to make these centers attractive. Some are beautiful old houses set in spacious grounds. Teachers look forward to a week or weekend there not only for the teaching help they receive, but also for the chance to meet colleagues in a relaxed and informal way, outside the pressures of the school where they work.

Many different organizations run the in-service courses. The local education authorities offer a number. The Department of Education and Science also gives some, as do colleges of education and universities. Only in a few of these courses do teachers receive academic credit for time devoted to this work. Some universities provide evening, weekend, and vacation courses leading to a degree, but these involve only a small number of teachers. The majority attend the short courses out of interest and a knowledge that they will gain professional credit within their school or local authority for attending. Over a quarter of all primary teachers in England attend some form of in-service course during each school year.

Local teachers' centers, usually run by the L.E.A.s, have been slower to grow in number than the residential centers. Only a few counties have viable local centers and none have enough to make them truly accessible to a large number of teachers; yet, local centers are a success where they have been well established. The courses offered by local centers may be one session affairs dealing with a restricted subject or evening gatherings stretching over a number of weeks. But the courses are not the paramount functions of the centers. Their main purpose is to give teachers from all over the authority a convenient place to meet and talk. Coffee and tea are available; often library collections are on hand. Children's work is on display. If the center is not too difficult for teachers to reach, it becomes a cheerful and often frequented gathering place. The centers do a great deal to break down the teacher's feeling of isolation. A teacher working innovatively, but alone, in a traditional school may find comfort in meeting another teacher who faces the same difficulties. Friendships are formed that benefit the exchange of ideas and thus, indirectly, the children in the classrooms.

MUSEUMS AND THE SCHOOLS

In addition to the regional developments in advisory services and teachers' centers, a third innovative force is appearing in some areas. Usually called the museum school service, this is an effort to offer school children and teachers the resources of regional museums and their staffs. These remarkable services provide objects for practical classroom use on a rotating basis and also contribute staff members who perform another type of advisory service in the area.

A museum truck delivering an order to a school might drop off some shards of Roman pottery, a model of a windmill, three examples of nineteenth-century agricultural hand implements, two large lengths of particularly beautiful hand-woven fabrics made for the service by a local weaver, a sample set of cups and mugs made by hand in a nearby pottery, and a stuffed and mounted red fox. All of these pieces will arrive safely packed in their own cartons and will usually be on loan to the school for two weeks. The objects are put on display in different classrooms, and the children are urged to touch, draw, observe, and write about them. The objects are often requested by teachers because they are related to a subject that is of interest to a particular class. In order to serve a useful function, objects have to be delivered fairly promptly. The museum school service has to have good relations with teachers and be able to fill their requests with as few delays or refusals as possible. Damage, although allowed for by the service, is usually minimal. Children are remarkably careful of the objects used in the schools.

These services also work to provide good surroundings for the children in the museum itself. In one local museum that we visited, rooms are made available to children and supplied with pads, paints, drawing paper, and all the needs of the classroom. A child can work at the museum; he need not view a case for a limited period, then climb back on a bus and return to school. In this particular museum, someone was on hand to help the children. A teacher could send five or six members of his class to the museum to work alone and keep the others in school. Items in the museum's permanent collection are there for the children to examine in ways that would not be open to them on a conventional museum trip.

The staffs of the best services sometimes act as ad hoc advisers, filling in for regular advisers when the museum staff is better informed or equipped to do the job. We observed two cases where museum staffs accompanied classes on their visits to sites of historical interest. The members of the museum service helped children and teachers with some limited excavation at the site, with the collection and identification of interesting objects, and with follow-up work in the classroom. A few museums extend this type of work and offer their own in-service courses to familiarize teachers with the range of opportunities available within the framework of the museum and its collections.

This type of service implies an unusual understanding of a museum's function. Rather than collect rare items, which could never be replaced if lost or broken, the school museum services commission craftsmen and artists to make articles of high quality and outstanding design. In some areas, a museum's influence has led to a resurgence of local crafts and an appreciation of forgotten art forms. Children and parents are surprised to learn, through the service, that a famous potter is living in the area, or that the county boasts a woman who creates beautiful hand-printed fabrics, using local dyes.

These small museums thus make an important contribution to the community as well as to the schools. Their collections are enhanced for the children by the fact that items can be handled, touched, and observed over a long period of time. The museums bring knowledge and material into schools that has often been unavailable, and they increase the child's sensory awareness through first-hand exposure to a variety of objects. They stimulate teachers to try new techniques and to explore different topics. The school which receives an unexpected shipment of animal skeletons, or a penny farthing bicycle, will find its students involved in a startling range of new interests.

Through advisory services, in-service training, school museum services, and other facilities, the local education authority makes many efforts to improve the quality of learning in its area. Where its services are most effective, they promote cooperation between teachers and foster a healthy, positive attitude toward change—relying on the capabilities of teachers throughout the area.

At the same time, there are other bodies which must cope with education at the national level. Their job is often more difficult, for they must avoid a messianic approach to change in order to encourage backward areas to move in a progressive direction; at the same time, they will want to encourage those few areas which have made enormous progress without making them overconfident or self-satisfied. A number of these national bodies, which have no parallel in American education, are worth consideration here.

THE SCHOOLS COUNCIL

The Schools Council for the Curriculum and Examinations, established in 1964, is a national body that aims to facilitate the flow of information at all levels of public education. It was originally established to coordinate new developments in the curriculum with those in examinations and has also dealt extensively with the extension of the school-leaving age to sixteen. It now sponsors research towards development of curriculum materials, coordinates innovative work that takes place throughout the country, and acts as a clearing house for new ideas.

The council is composed of primary and secondary school teachers, local education authority representatives, university staff, and all other major interest groups in English education. About four hundred people serve on the council at one time, including the governing body of eighty members and the membership of various specialized committees. This means that the council is composed of members drawn from all over the country. A gathering of the council greatly enhances all types of communication.

While the majority of its work is aimed at secondary schools (desperately in need of its help), the council is well-known for its work in developing science and math materials for primary children. It has also produced materials for teaching French and has a number of other projects under way at the present time. In each of these areas, it has made a valuable contribution. In science and mathematics, booklets encourage work which is interdisciplinary in nature and conducive to informal classroom practices. The booklets seldom tell the teacher *how* to teach something, but provide him with many concrete ideas and suggestions.

The French material, called *En Avant*, presents more difficulties. It is a project which is hard to teach in any but a formal setting. This causes many conflicts in an informal classroom. In general, there are not enough teachers who are qualified to teach French. Many teachers feel that teaching French in primary school is of questionable importance. The money and materials might be better spent on the development of projects for non-English speaking children (Indians, Pakistanis, and Cypriots, to mention a few), who desperately need qualified teachers to help them in schools. The Schools Council has a project under way in this area, but much more needs to be done.

Aside from developing materials, the Schools Council has encouraged the development of teachers' centers and residential weekend and vacation programs in many fields. Much of the important work in this field has been done in conjunction with L.E.A.s.

Some teachers are concerned that the Schools Council will become an arm of the central government and impose curriculum. Teachers have spoken to us of their alarm at the widespread and sometimes indiscriminate use of *En Avant*. Others have complained about the standardization that could result from strict use of *Science 5/13* when it becomes available to all primary schools. These concerns are very important, but they are not typical of the way most teachers react to the organization. Because so many teachers are directly involved in the Schools Council's work, they are less likely to feel that it is a higher authority with little relation to the schools. On the contrary, its projects often originate in classroom work, and they are certainly tested extensively in the schools. Many teachers are intrigued by the Schools Council's work and have been helped enormously by their science and mathematics projects. It is also important to consider the implications of these projects for the weaker teacher. While they are never called "teacher proof" (as they might be in the United States), the Schools Council's projects can benefit and help the teacher who finds it hard to cope with informal methods and who has fewer resources of his own to draw upon.

Most teachers would probably agree with the council's former secretary, Geoffrey Caston, who has written:

> . . . the Council has no authority over teachers. It may—and I hope it does—sometimes carry a certain amount of weight of professional consensus, and a great deal of the kind of authority which comes from organized knowledge. But it cannot instruct anyone to do anything. To my mind . . . this is a great source of strength.[6]

While their title suggests immense power to command and regulate what they see, Her Majesty's Inspectorate of Schools is generally a forward-looking and creative group of individuals. Their role is unique to England. Their appointments are confirmed by the Queen, and they work within the framework of the Department of Education and Science, technically reporting directly to the Secretary of State.

H.M.I.s, as they are called, may enter any school and observe the teaching, check on the standards of education throughout the building, and assess the school for its ability to provide an adequate learning experience for the children. When the group was first established in 1839, they were licensed to grant money to individual schools, based upon examinations of the children. A bad school received less money than a good one, as a result of their evaluation. Their annual reports to schools were often brutally critical. Mathew Arnold, a famous H.M.I., reporting on a school in 1859, said: "The institution has sunk and is sinking."[7] Although this was not an uncommon approach for an H.M.I. to take in the nineteenth century, it would be a rare attitude to find today.

The force of nearly five hundred men and women is composed of experienced teachers and educators, in the fields of both primary and secondary education. They are in contact with teachers throughout England. Although they now have no financial control over schools and no authority to require change in any way, their influence is substantial. They live in the area that is assigned to them, and thus have access to both L.E.A.s and colleges of education, though they are independent of both these institutions.

John Blackie, a former Chief Inspector for Primary Education and an innovative and energetic member of the Inspectorate for many years, described the function of the H.M.I. in his helpful book *Inside the Primary School:*

> First and most obviously the teachers gain from having their work seen by, and being able to discuss it with, someone who is a teacher himself, who has seen the work of many other teachers and schools and who is not an employee of the L.E.A. . . .[The Inspectorate] is very proud of its traditions of independent professional judgment and of its high standards. . . . [The H.M.I.] does not go round preaching a doctrine. . . . He works by influence not by authority.[8]

The H.M.I.s in recent years have had a marked influence on the changes that have taken place in education. Although they are not primarily responsible for change, they can encourage it, and watch for problems. They can try to keep officials and teachers up to date on recent developments and can smooth over some difficulties that arise within local education authorities. It is a tribute to English thinking on education that a force of five hundred people can continue to act as observers without having a major vested interest or a solely administrative function within the system.

After a year spent in English schools, it is clear to us that the talented teacher is essential to the innovative process. Unlike many of his counterparts in America, the experienced teacher in England plays a substantial role in the creation of new techniques. His participation in change, especially at the infant level, has been evident throughout this century and is spreading rapidly to other levels of the system. Many new ideas about teaching originate in the classroom, among the children. Bodies such as the Inspectorate, the advisory services, and the Schools Council are composed mainly of exciting teachers and heads, who continue to make valuable contributions to children as they spread ideas from school to school.

Change in the American system is entirely different. With the exception of a few projects (such as those produced by the Educational Development Center, for instance), new ideas for the curriculum in the United States are developed away from the teacher and the classroom. They are usually produced in textbook form. G. W. Bassett, whose recent book compares the innovative processes in England and America, says of change in the United States:

> In all this activity, the dominant figures appear to be the politicians, the professors, the research and curriculum specialists, the engineers, and the publishers, rather than the teachers. The forces working towards change come for the most part from outside the schools.[9]

A great many new ideas for education in America originate in the universities. While this type of research draws on the talents of the brightest mathematicians, scientists, and linguists, the danger arises that great gaps may develop between the teams in the universities and the children in the classrooms. In addition, the men and women who are engaged in this research deal with individual subject matter and are usually not concerned with the curriculum as a whole. The mathematician is not interested in the language development or the social studies program that will be taught alongside his sixth-grade math project. He is concerned with the success of his mathematics textbook and with the value of his approach to the subject.

In England the opposite is true. Innovation, even in

subject matter, is largely developed in the context of the entire curriculum. Nuffield Mathematics, for instance, attempts to relate the learning of math to other classroom activities and to child development. This approach is reinforced by Jean Piaget's work, which emphasizes that the child needs to relate many different aspects of learning to one another if he is to progress logically from one stage of development to the next. The child is less likely to understand life as a whole if he is constantly exposed to learning which is fragmented into isolated subjects.

Thus, the music adviser from an L.E.A. does not present the teacher with a textbook for teaching music to the children. He looks at the teacher's classroom and approach to learning. He observes the children and suggests ways that music might relate to the rest of the work taking place. His suggestions will doubtless vary from teacher to teacher; his ideas about music will be closely related to his thoughts on the process of learning as a whole.

On the other hand, the lack of money for research at the university level in England does keep some people with special talents from contributing to primary education. Because the agencies in England are so adaptable and still so close to the classroom, the university researcher could well become an important member of innovative bodies. Educators in England have expressed frustration at the lack of money which now prevents this type of exchange from taking place.

There is a further development in America which illustrates the prevalent attitude toward the teacher's contribution to educational changes. This is the manufacture of "teacher-proof" materials. Where American researchers attempt to produce a syllabus that even the worst teacher can manage, (with the exception, perhaps, of projects such as Elementary Science Study), English materials often require good teachers. The new curricula in England leave most of the decisions up to the teacher. The English seem to expect the best from their teachers—whereas a teacher-proof program implies that the system has little faith in the average teacher's ability to initiate creative, productive learning. While not all of Great Britain's teachers are able to respond as the system might hope, it is our feeling that a positive approach to human potential is always better than a negative one and will often produce finer results.

The agencies of change in England can be flexible and oriented toward the classroom because they all possess a certain degree of discretion. There is no strict hierarchy of agencies in England the way there is in America. Advisers, H.M.I.s, head teachers, and staffs are all responsible to someone—but not in a way that inhibits their creativity. The local education authority and the Department of Education and Science, for example, contribute financially to the Schools Council, yet they are not subservient to it, nor does the Council have to answer to them. Teachers may receive the Schools Council material, but they are not required to use it if they feel it is unsuited to their children. The innovative agencies in England have different functions, and the relationships that have developed between them allow for maximum flexibility. They insure that change at the primary level keeps its sights on the most productive and imaginative sources of innovation: the teachers and the children in the schools.

CHAPTER EIGHT

Years of Reform

IN THE SPRING of 1970 Great Britain celebrated her first one hundred years of universal state education. Local governments across the country created displays and wrote essays marking the centennial. A few brave schools opened their doors to the public for two or three days. The central government organized a national exhibit, which opened in London and later toured the country, to show England what its education would be like in the seventies. Educators looked ahead to the future of the system and its long-term effects on children and adults.

The centennial was also important for the chance it gave teachers, parents, and educators to note the numerous gains that had been made since the institution of compulsory education in 1870. Teachers were reminded of the freedoms they had achieved. Children constructed "The Classroom of 1870" and were amazed at its physical and intellectual restrictions.

More importantly, the country realized that the aims and purposes of education in 1970 were radically different from those of a hundred years earlier. In the late nineteenth century (and well into the twentieth in some areas), the schools supported by the state had a single purpose: to better prepare the working class to serve the country. Children were seen in terms of their future economic potential. Society assumed that a child would only reach a certain level of achievement—unless, of course, he happened to be born into a privileged family. In that case, he would attend a private school, a university, and then enter the country's ruling elite.

Ideas of this sort are hard to extinguish, both in England and in the United States. The class system is still very strong in Great Britain, but the attitudes toward children's education have certainly improved since 1870. Most state supported schools, especially those at the primary level, are increasingly concerned with personal development and individual needs. The state school is gradually losing its former stigma as a catch-all for the working class, especially in those areas which lead the country in innovative practices.

While educators, in their reappraisal of schools during the centennial, were interested in making an assessment of past achievements, observers from other countries wondered what forces had radically changed some English primary schools in such disparate areas of England. Although much of this change has been haphazard and dependent upon the initiative of individuals, education in England has moved slowly in a progressive direction. On the whole, educators have managed to avoid rapid swings of the pendulum, although a substantial minority of English primary schools, both infant and junior, remain strictly traditional and ignorant of changes taking place around them. Despite the existence of a large number of old-fashioned schools, no one can deny that a few English primary schools are (as one optimist put it) "among the best in the world." Yet the question that occurs again and again is: how did it happen in England?

While there is no overall pattern that characterizes the history of educational changes in England, one of the most important factors has been the position of the teacher. As we mentioned in the last two chapters, the country relies on its talented teachers to keep education in a continuous state of reappraisal and renewal. Inspired teachers in England have been responsible for the positive growth in education that has taken place since the beginning of the century. Teachers have possessed substantial freedom since 1898, when the system of payment by results and external examination was abolished in the schools. Until that time, a teacher was paid according to the number of pupils who were successful in passing certain exams. When this practice ended, a few teachers realized that they could develop a curriculum that was better suited to the children in their classrooms.

The existence of the infant school in England has also facilitated new developments. As we have indicated, many of the important changes in education have had their roots in work with five- to seven-year-olds. There is a long tradition of separation between this age group and other children. Even in the days of "all age" schools (taking children from five to fourteen), the infants formed a separate department. The acceptance of different methods for younger children was a great help to those early pioneers who wanted to teach imaginatively. These schools were free from the threat of external examinations and often attracted young staff members who were eager to experiment. In addition, infant-school teachers were trained for work with nursery-age children—an asset in that they learned to value a freer atmosphere and to respect the child's need for productive play.

Infant schools have not always been lauded. In fact, they were once dreary institutions which educated far too many children in the same way at the same time. One method of learning was considered good enough for all. Photographs of infant and junior schools taken early in the century reveal rows of children seated on wooden benches, rising in tiers away from the central figure: the teacher. There is no doubt that infant schools have made enormous progress since then and that many changed when other parts of the system seemed sterile and motionless.

The fact that English infant children enter the infant school at five—before they would start school in most of Europe and earlier than the age for first grade in the United States—is not the most important factor in the schools' successes. Neither does the five- to seven- or eight-year-old grouping guarantee an informal and successful experience for the children. As proof of this, observers point to infant schools in Wales, where education has proved generally poor and without innovation for years.

In order to understand some of the early reforms that reached some English infant schools and later the junior schools, we can look briefly at a few of the men and women who influenced, directly or indirectly, the progressive thinking that took place in a few schools that first tried informed child-centered practices.

Throughout the course of this century, teachers in England and America have been influenced at different times by numerous theories of education. A great deal is now known about the way children grow, develop, and learn to think. In both countries, educators have tried to organize a growing body of educational research and apply it to work in the classroom.

Infant-school teachers in England have long been concerned with the complex nature of young children and their patterns of learning. In many cases, the inspired work of a few early infant teachers was reinforced by the theories of learning which sometimes found their way into the schools.

One of the earliest and quite influential theorists was Friedrich Froebel, whose disciples started kindergartens in England and America. The effect of his thinking on English schools can still be seen in good classrooms—although few teachers are consciously aware of it.

Considering how little scientific data about the child was available in Froebel's time, his understanding of children's nature was profound. He was one of the first educators who was sensitive to the value of play for the young child. While both Froebel and his followers conceived of play as largely a teacher-directed activity, the realization of its importance to learning was a breakthrough in educational thought.

Froebel's beliefs about children were deeply religious. He sought the complete unity of man with nature and felt that one must start with the young child in order to achieve this perfect state. He took the children for long walks and used the outdoors as his classroom. (Hence his use of the term "kindergarten" for his school.) The idea that children learn by understanding the world around them is still very important in English primary schools.

Froebel was often misunderstood. He had invented a number of "gifts"—learning games and toys for specific purposes. As is often the case, many teachers used the apparatus with little or no understanding of the ideas behind it. Froebel felt that children were "not to be schooled, but freely developed,"[1] a concept which ran contrary to Victorian ideas and could not be accepted by most teachers. Others, however, trained by Froebelians, were able to put his ideas into practice. The existence of two excellent training institutions in England, established in his name, is an indication of the long-lasting attraction of his theories.

Unfortunately, many educators in England and America have ignored one of Froebel's main interests, namely the preschool-age child. While his theories have been successfully applied in primary schools, they have been neglected in early education which is sorely in need of attention in both countries. Nursery schools or other public facilities for preschool education have never been available to large numbers of children in England. Until recently there had been no extensive pressure to establish them, despite years of urging by some prominent educators.

Maria Montessori was another pioneer whose influence was felt in England in the early part of this century. Like Froebel, she had worked with some children younger than primary school age, yet teachers in England applied her findings to the five- to seven-year-old range. Montessori played an important role in the development of teaching techniques for young children. Dorothy Gardner, an educator who has watched and encouraged change in primary schools over a number of years, feels that Montessori's contribution to education was to leave much of the learning up to the child. While the teacher regularized the work and decided that the child must do step one before step two, the child— not the teacher—was at the center of the classroom. Contrary to Froebel's belief, however, Montessori felt that play was entirely extraneous to learning and that such materials as clay, paint, and water had no place in school. Teachers in England came into contact with Montessori's work through articles, books, workshops, and word of mouth. Some of her games were introduced in a few scattered classrooms but never gained wide acceptance.

Together, Froebel and Montessori offered a great deal to the teacher of young children. It is impossible, however, to measure the extent of this influence in the early part of the century. The Plowden Report comments:

> A considerable body of liberal thinking on the education of children was available to teachers. Rousseau, Pestalozzi, Froebel, Whitehead, Dewey, Montessori and Rachel MacMillan, to mention only a few, had all written on lines that encouraged change and innovation. Yet it may be doubted whether the direct influence of these or of any other writers was great. It was rare to find teachers who had given much time to the study of educational theory, even in their training college days.[2]

There were a number of important developments in the 1930's and 1940's which had a profound effect on educational thought in England. One was the increase of knowledge about intelligence tests. Such tests came into use in England shortly after their large-scale use in the United States during the First World War. The implication of the intelligence tests, as seen by many teachers, was that children were even more different than had been thought and demanded individual techniques according to their abilities.

Another major event in the years between the two World Wars was the publication of the Hadow Report, dealing in three sections with secondary, junior, and infant schools. The volume which concerned children of junior age was released in 1931 and drew national attention for a number of reasons. For the first time, the country considered the problems of the middle range of education and proposals were made for the establishment of separate junior schools.

The Hadow Report identified children in classrooms as individuals with individual needs. The members of the Hadow committee were concerned with every aspect of a child's education and urged teachers to teach children about life as a whole. This progressive document reinforced the work of innovative teachers and caused others to consider the implications of its forward-looking ideas. The later volume, published in 1933, dealt largely with infant schools. It stressed the importance of the early years and encouraged teachers who were already engaged in progressive practice.

Like many reports of its kind, Hadow's effects were immediate in only a few areas and negligible in those authorities which needed help most. Many of its organizational recommendations—such as the establishment of junior schools—quickly took effect. However, important aspects of the committee's report, including urgings that the schools make greater efforts to understand the nature of the child, were neglected for many years.

The writings of John Dewey were also of substantial interest in England. Although his works did not form the cornerstone of a national movement, as they did in the United States, his books received substantial circulation and acclaim. Proponents of his thinking came from America to speak and to write. Some English schools adopted progressive labels, but there was little of the negative aspect of progressivism—the rejection of all prior educational practice—that was seen in the United States.

The writings of the English psychologist Susan Isaacs, which appeared throughout the 1930's, took some time to reach large segments of practicing teachers, but a number of people were quickly and deeply affected by her work. Dorothy Gardner has observed that the timing of Susan Isaacs' arrival in the fields of education and psychology was fortunate for all concerned. Isaacs was able to draw heavily on the work of John Dewey that was applicable to English education and to make his ideas more widely known. She extracted much of the most pertinent material from Froebel and Montessori. More importantly, she brought to her work perceptive ideas about the ways in which children learn. She presented new arguments for the value of play. One of Isaacs' strengths was that she did not prescribe a classroom "method" to teachers. Instead, she presented them with knowledge about learning and insisted that the teacher find the right way to use this knowledge with children. Her understanding of children was supported by carefully documented research which largely proved the success of newer methods geared to individual needs.

Susan Isaacs brought to her work the experience gained at the Malting House School in Cambridge. There, beginning in the fall of 1924, children from the age of three to seven played and learned in an informal setting under the guidance of Isaacs and others.[3] The children were encouraged to pursue their interests, to work with a variety of tools, and to do this with other children, developing friendships and working out difficulties. The activities at the Malting House School were carefully recorded, with entire dialogues between children often taken down by hand. The data collected at the school proved invaluable to Isaacs' later work.

Susan Isaacs' research also influenced the work of the Swiss psychologist and epistemologist Jean Piaget during the 1930's. Partly because of his interest in Isaacs' emphasis on the value of play, he increasingly used interview techniques with children which took notice of their natural interests and tended to examine the development of the whole child.[4]

In the more immediately applicable fields of art and

crafts, the work of two other individuals began to influence teachers in the 1930's. Marion Richardson, working in Birmingham at the time of the First World War, encouraged the use of a variety of paints and large paper and permitted children to paint what interested them. She urged children to take the time to complete a work they cared about and allowed them to abandon a less successful piece. All of this was out of keeping with the formal art work employed in most schools, for copying was then the accepted mode of both drawing and writing.

Robin Tanner's work with children in art and crafts was also unusual and virtually unacceptable in the eyes of many teachers in the late 1920's and 1930's. Working first in London, he aided children to pursue handcrafts, such as block and linecut printing, forms of dyeing, italic handwriting, and woodworking. He encouraged a wide range of expression in all art forms and, after becoming an H.M.I. in 1935, was able to expose teachers to his work. Through Tanner, as well as Marion Richardson, many teachers began to recognize opportunities for children to express themselves in ways other than writing or speaking. The success of a number of teachers—with the help of H.M.I.s, local authority advisers, and some published material—led to the spread of arts and crafts work to many schools in the years preceding the Second World War.

Much of this work, however, was interrupted or altered by the devastating experience of the war, which brought both a breakdown in education, and, at the same time, a forward-looking Education Act and re-evaluation of the educational structure. During the war, many schools closed and a number were destroyed. Children were evacuated to rural areas, where teachers suddenly had to face large classes of dissimilar children.

Many found that the only way to cope was to work with children individually and make the curriculum flexible. Materials had to be acquired as best they could, and supplies of many items disappeared. When textbooks and readers wore out, they were seldom replaced, forcing even book-bound teachers to improvise. After the war, new buildings and the influx of discharged armed service personnel to the teaching profession added to the ferment. Many teachers were open to new ideas about children and eager to experiment.

Since the end of the war, the growth in teachers' awareness of learning theories has been sizeable. While the work of innovators such as Froebel and Montessori had effect in scattered schools, the recent knowledge of how children learn has been better disseminated. One reason for the acceptance of certain theories in England may be that teachers play an important role in theoretical research. Susan Isaacs, for example, drew a great deal of research material from large samples of infant classrooms, not from isolated demonstration or experimental schools. Her written descriptions are thoroughly familiar to infant-school teachers. But this is not the only factor involved in teachers' interests in theoretical material.

Teachers in England are intrigued with the work of developmental psychologists because it tends to confirm what they have discovered about children. A large number of teachers in England contend that children must be treated individually and that each child learns in his own way. They believe they will be more successful if the child is allowed to proceed with certain tasks when he is ready, regardless of the teacher's timetable.

Of the many developmental psychologists whose writings are available to teachers in England, the individual most often mentioned is Jean Piaget.

Although Piaget has never directed his work toward education in the traditional sense, his theories on stages of development and the unique growth of each child have been attractive to educators. Some of his work has centered on learning tests that relate directly to work in schools. Although few teachers with whom we spoke had read any of Piaget's work, a number were familiar with interpretations aimed at teachers. An interest in applying Piaget's work to primary education has been evident in England since the late 1950's, and a large number of books and articles have appeared, dealing with applications of his work to the classroom.

The link between English educators and the researchers in Geneva is sufficiently strong that a team under Piaget's direction is preparing "Check-up Guides" for the Nuffield Mathematics Project. These, the Project contends, "will provide 'check-ups' on the children's progress. The traditional tests are difficult to administer in the new atmosphere of individual discovery and so our intention is to replace these by individual check-ups for individual children."[5]

This work along developmental lines, with Piaget's name in the forefront, is in keeping with ideas that have been fostered in English education since the late 1920's. English educators have not been captivated by behaviorist theory as many Americans have. One indication is that various forms of behavioral objectives have attracted almost no attention in England. These objectives, requiring predetermination of the behavior, or response, expected from the child, have interested many American educators over the last six years.

Among other objections, educators in England with

whom we talked believed that it would be very difficult to design behavioral objectives suitable for use in an informal setting. We also encountered the argument that a behavioral objective presupposed a teacher-directed classroom with little or no chance for the child to set objectives on his own. A situation such as this would be contrary to the aims of a number of schools in England.

Many of the ideas and practical experiences that influenced a number of English primary schools were drawn together in a document published in 1967. Commonly called the Plowden Report (mentioned in the introduction to this book), it was the product of the Central Advisory Council for Education in England and was commissioned in 1963 by the Secretary of State for Education and Science. Although it was not granted the status of a government white paper, the report had wide publicity and the advantage of government publication.

The Plowden Report dealt with a remarkable range of issues that concerned children. It spoke to the problems of preschool care and learning and dealt with parents, staffing, teacher training, and research, as well as the school's social, economic, and governmental aspects. While its major concern was with primary education, it has had implications for education at all levels.

The report has had a profound effect on primary schools throughout the country. Because of the breadth of its recommendations, large portions of it are applicable to all schools, in England and elsewhere. Its progressive intent has caused teachers and heads to seize upon it to provide ideas and to reinforce debate about a child-centered curriculum. Undoubtedly, excerpts from it have been used to support arguments that the council itself would not have accepted, but in the main, it has been a very positive force which has influenced a wide spectrum of people concerned with primary education.

A report such as Plowden has substantial long-term influence. Many of its recommendations have been adopted by schools and enforced by the central government. With its second volume of research and surveys, it is the most comprehensive study of English primary education that has been undertaken for some years. Plowden built on some of the best thinking of the Hadow Report, completed in 1933, and has gone beyond it in many fields. Because Plowden was a major study undertaken by prominent individuals, and because it will not be duplicated in the near future, teachers and interested parents read it as a matter of course. Head teachers often refer to it in conversation and display substantial knowledge of its contents. Copies of the report, tattered and marked from extensive use, may be found on staff room shelves.

Although the Plowden Report deals with English education, much of it is applicable to education in other countries. Of particular note for Americans is Part Two, "The Growth of the Child," a sensitive survey of child development, which points to aspects of particular value to teachers. Later discussions of the importance of the home and concrete recommendations for improved contacts between home and school are likewise helpful in countries other than England. Another important section surveys problems of preschool care in England, trying to estimate future needs and making proposals for action.

Any teacher, administrator, or parent might benefit from a careful reading of Part Five, "The Children in the Schools," which examines freer curricula, the child's position in the school community, and the problems of special education. This part also considers most aspects of the curriculum individually. There are worthwhile sections on mathematics, reading, various art forms, and physical education, surveying some of the best work in primary schools. Parts of these sections are limited or have little bearing outside England, but read selectively, this portion of the report is of great use.

Plowden leaves nothing untouched in the realm of primary education. Teacher training, staffing, the construction of buildings, and ideas for further research are all dealt with at length. Volume Two provides appendices of research and surveys carried out or collated by the Council. Although at first glance, Plowden appears to be a document for the researcher, it is more than that. For example, the section called "The Social Services and Primary Education" remains the most concise discussion of services available to children and families in England, and it makes recommendations worthy of consideration in most western countries.

Plowden's most impressive contribution is undoubtedly the expression of an objective and forward-looking educational philosophy which is based on concrete knowledge of what children are, rather than on an irrelevant dream of what they should be. The Plowden Report lauds those schools which recognize the importance of the child's present experience. It should be read by anyone who cares deeply about the growth and happiness of children.

In order to create primary schools of the caliber found in a number of English communities and endorsed by the Plowden Report, thousands of individuals have committed their time and energy to changing the forms of education already in existence. Many different forces have been at work, and each school has faced its own particular set of problems. Schools and teachers have not been involved in any organized national movement on the part of administrators, academicians, or others concerned with the schools. The existence of the infant school, the work of small groups of innovators, and the massive disruptions of the Second World War have all contributed, separately, to the emergence of a number of exceptional schools for young children.

Those schools which have met with success have done so with local, not national, help. The various education acts that have touched upon the primary schools in the last one hundred years have at times encouraged change but have never acted directly to bring it about. The efforts of local advisers, Chief Education Officers, and groups of head teachers have been vital to the promotion of change. Nonetheless, in many schools children still receive an education that would be familiar to late nineteenth-century teachers. Elsewhere, schools have been modified and teachers use all the latest slogans while helping the children very little. Teachers and schools subject to these many forces have not all responded in positive ways. A number, however, have added their own particular talents to the innovations already under way in the schools. Some of the finest examples of this sort of change are discussed in the following chapters, which deal with new developments in the curriculum that now form some of the most outstanding examples of success in English primary schools.

CHAPTER NINE

Physical Education and the Art of Movement

PHYSICAL EDUCATION PLAYS an important role in the curricula of many English primary schools. It is a many faceted subject which involves far more than games and the development of coordination skills. The most exciting aspects of physical education in England are, first, the use of simple, multipurpose apparatus in the halls of the primary schools and, second, movement education, which employs forms of modern dance for children from five to eleven. Through the movement work in particular, teachers have found a new source of knowledge about individual children.

John Blackie, for many years one of Her Majesty's Inspectors, has observed classrooms throughout the country and sums up the aims of a movement class this way:

> . . . it begins by being an exploration of the body's capacity for movement, heavy and light, large and small, fast and slow, with the whole body involved. . . . As time goes on, control of the body develops and the children are able to perform a very wide range of movements, with confidence and grace, both singly, in pairs and in groups, the pairs and groups forming and disintegrating as the movement demands.[1]

In the late fall, we visited schools in the West Riding of Yorkshire. In small, depressed mining towns, rural communities, and industrial suburbs, schools are working imaginatively in many fields. One such school is situated in an ex-mining area near the large city of Leeds. From a hillside near the school, one can see a vast industrial wasteland. Iron foundries, chemical plants, and a myriad display of smokestacks and machinery rise up from an open plain and stretch for miles toward Leeds.

In the town itself, we felt trapped and enclosed. Rows of identical houses border the roads, some doorsteps no more than two feet from the wheels of our car. Each house seemed to lean heavily on the next, all the way to the school, which was itself a victim of cramped spaces. The classrooms, designed by a Victorian architect with a passion for high ceilings and little floor space, were miserably overcrowded, having forty children in nearly every one.

A hall in the school that once was used for many purposes was now filled with the echoes of small voices. A class of infant children was temporarily installed there, awaiting the arrival of a new "temporary" classroom. In the school's cloakroom, at the end of long rows of coats and boots, the dinner ladies had only a small space in which to prepare the school lunches brought in by the catering service.

Outside on the asphalt playground were two temporary buildings housing two classes of juniors. In one, run by a Welshman, the children had found a release from the physical restrictions of the town and their lives.

When we entered the room, coming in from the outside, we found a movement class under way. Both boys and girls wore shorts and T-shirts, and despite the November weather, they were clearly warm and unencumbered. Desks, chairs, tables, and equipment were neatly stacked in the corners, leaving the floor open. For lack of enough space, the boys sat on the floor, while the girls danced, exploring the spaces around them, moving between and around one another. There was music playing, acting as a catalyst that sparked them off. Yet, no child followed the beat in any formal pattern. Each girl's movement was unique, her own interpretation grew out of the music and was expressed with every part of her body. After a few minutes, the teacher stopped the girls, who flopped down on the floor, panting and out of breath.

"Would anyone like to comment on what any particular girl was doing just now?" The teacher aimed his question at the boys, who had been absorbed in watching the girls as they moved.

"I liked Jenny," said one boy.

"What did you notice about her movements?"

"She was leading with her elbow all the time."

"Well then Jenny, can you show us what you were doing?" the teacher asked.

Jenny danced alone in the middle of the group, her elbows leading her body in slow circles across the floor. Her face was calm and serene; she was completely lost in her movements and had to be asked twice, gently, to stop. The class talked further about what she had been doing. They felt her circles were "slow and smooth." They liked the way her arms curved to shape her circles.

"Anyone else among the girls that you'd like to watch?"

"Yes, Betsy," someone said.

"What was she doing?"

"She was using her toes on the floor."

Betsy's short body pulled up toward the ceiling and balanced on her toes as she moved in a series of short, sharp steps across the room. All the children pointed to the difference between the two girls; Betsy's jerky, stretched quality compared to the low, weaving circles that Jenny had used. Both had been supported by the same piece of music, yet their movements were completely dissimilar. Each had revealed something of herself to her peers, to the teacher, and to us.

The boys moved onto the floor and found different ways to respond to the music. The teacher gave them time to experiment, reminding them to find spaces and to spread out on the floor. When they had found patterns they could repeat, he stopped them and asked that they present a finished sequence of movements.

The girls were full of opinions. They liked Julian because he "went up light and came down heavy." Julian's dance certainly fit these words. He flung himself lightly up toward the ceiling, poised for a split second in midair, and then dropped to a low, heavy crouch with hands, elbows, knees, and feet pressed to the floor. He was a big child, but when he left the floor he seemed weightless and free. He was able to repeat his pattern two or three times in the space of the room, and we were aware of the deep feeling which his body expressed. We later learned that Julian was having difficulty in other subjects. In the expression of joy that lit his face, we recognized success. There was no need to grade Julian's performance. It was magnificent.

This class—although unusual for the contrast it presented between the crowded school and the expansive movements of the children—is not unique. Its like may be found in schools in a number of counties. Imaginative movement sessions are far more unusual for juniors, however, than for infant-school children. Aside from the physical and emotional advantages of movement for all ages, observation of the children can be a substantial help to the teacher.

In one instance a child who was withdrawn and sometimes sullen in the classroom broke into exciting and expansive movement in the hall. His teacher, surprised at seeing this repeatedly, tried to determine what was weighing upon him in the classroom. With the help of other members of the staff, she finally established that this boy felt terribly threatened by reading and was constantly insecure in the classroom because of it. Through a combination of special help with reading and encouragement with other activities, the teachers helped this boy to treat the rest of his school day with the same interest that he treated movement. In other situations, teachers have reported that they discovered difficulties with coordination and problems in communication that they felt they would have missed had it not been for movement classes.

Much of the valuable work taking place in English movement classes today had its origins in the theories and teaching of Rudolph Laban (although influences have also come from Martha Graham, Heinya Holm, and others). Laban was a Czech dancer who first formulated his theories of movement while watching men and women in factories. During the build-up of Nazi power in Germany, he emigrated to England, where he continued to develop and explore uses of his movement theory in education. His work had substantial influence in some schools. Teachers today do not rely on his techniques alone, any more than they rely on strict methods in other parts of the curriculum, but his basic ideas are apparent in much of what takes place.

Laban feared that the mechanization of industry would destroy man's soul and depersonalize the world. He felt that man's natural urge to move should be developed and strengthened in order to offset the pressures and power of technology; that movement was a common denominator uniting men engaged in thousands of unrelated occupations. He viewed dance as "the basic art of man," giving all participants the chance to rediscover spontaneity and a feeling of freedom. [2]

Laban believed that the movements of dance and drama had their origin in movements that are central to the everyday work of men. On stage or in the classroom, the child or adult exploring dance was using everyday actions, but in a different context, in new and unusual ways. For Laban, movement was "a means of communication between people, because all our forms of expression—speaking, writing, singing—are carried by the flow of movement." [3]

In his book *Modern Educational Dance,* Laban proposed that schools use movement as an essential part of the curriculum. One of his important contributions in this discussion was his recognition of the child's natural urge to dance, an awareness that fit well with many British teachers' belief that the most productive and meaningful learning comes when the teacher utilizes and develops the natural assets of his pupils. While this is true in many other areas of the curriculum, it is perhaps most obvious in the movement class.

Some teachers in England argue that a child's capacity for moving and for language is the basis of his equality with other children. Diana Jordan, who has worked on movement with teachers for many years, points out that the child comes to school with five years of experience in movement. [4] Much of his early learning has been directly or indirectly facilitated by movement, and he enters school already equipped with bodily skills which constitute a wealth of resources for the teacher to foster and develop.

Both Jordan and Laban emphasize that it is the school's duty to encourage the growth of skills in movement without destroying the child's original spontaneity, a conviction inherent in much of what takes place in a good school, be it creative writing, describing a science experiment, or making a collage. The teacher must be aware of the child's abilities, recognize his talents as well as his areas of deficiency, and develop his interests and skills while allowing the child's own personality and strengths to emerge as paramount in what he is doing. In movement as in other pursuits, the most delicate understanding of each child is required. The teacher must know when to interfere, when to watch, when to initiate new directions, when to encourage the child, and when to suggest an alternative technique.

Laban's words of advice to the infant-school teacher were "guide them through suggestion."[5] He had a good understanding of the attainments possible for five- to seven-year-olds, and he divided his recommendation to teachers into three levels: infants, juniors, and secondary school. He felt that the child from the age of five to seven needed to develop an understanding of what his entire body was capable of doing so that he would increase his overall bodily awareness. In addition, he wrote, "the child should first learn to use space imaginatively, before making acquaintance with the regularities of space in floor patterns or set directional movements. . . . Dance training from its earliest stages is principally concerned with teaching the child to live, move, and express itself in the media which govern its life, the most important of which is the child's own flow of movement."[6]

At the infant stage, Laban proposed that the child should be introduced to the concepts of weight, time, and space. These are as essential to beginning reading or mathematics as they are to learning the use of one's own body and are part of most good primary school curricula, whether or not movement is taught. In movement, grasping these concepts involves many processes, including an awareness of one's body and the many positions and shapes it can assume—that is, whether the shape the body takes on is wide or narrow, high or low. Another concept involves the relationship of the body to the spaces in the room, or where one is in relation to the floor, the walls, the door.

In one school, watching two infant classes at work, we were able to see the differences in the children's understanding of space based upon their levels of development. The younger group, five-year-olds, were unable to spread themselves out on the floor although the hall was spacious. They bunched together at one end of the room and were constantly bumping into each other. Even when spaced by their teacher, they seemed to have a magnetic attraction to one another and would soon be huddled in a tightly knit, moving group.

On the other hand, the older children spread out across the room. When moving, they were able to run, twist, and jump in the air without collisions, conscious not only of their neighbors, but aware also of the four walls. A child would look eagerly toward an empty space and then run to use it.

Laban felt that an understanding of these concepts should lead to a more complex appreciation of dance on the part of the junior-age child. Movement for juniors should build on a growing consciousness of their bodies in space and should encourage the child to think of parts of his body in isolation. A junior should be able to understand rhythms, to repeat an improvised dance pattern (a task which an infant-school child might find difficult), and to develop a feeling for the deep roots that language, drama, and music have in dance.

Diana Jordan also outlines these basic goals for children. What she says about the purpose of movement is central to what we saw in many classes and crucial to an understanding of why movement is considered a natural and obvious part of the curriculum:

> If the body is also the image of personality, and surely it is, opportunity must be given for this whole personality to grow. . . . Personality has its outlet through mind, feeling, and imagination in the expressive movements of the body, both spontaneous and disciplined.
>
> The purpose of this activity of mind, imagination, and body is that the child shall experience one-ness with himself and with his fellows, freedom to be an individual as well as a richer member of a group of individuals.[7]

Jordan sums up the basic aims of movement in the schools as mastery of one's own weight, development of the power to move freely through the air and on the floor, discovery of other ways to move, understanding the different parts of the body and how they move independently, and grasping the quality of movement through energy, speed, and direction.[8] For juniors, she adds the goals of beginning communication through movement, a growing self-awareness, the ability to reproduce a sequence of movement, and an understanding of the relationship between music and dance.

In the cramped classroom near Leeds we had seen

many of these factors at work. These junior-school children had reached the stage of being able to invent entirely individual patterns of movement which they could recall and repeat for the group. This unusual form of learning involves what is known as kinesthetic memory.

The children had obviously discovered a great deal about the relation of their bodies to the space around them, for no one in that small building collided, although there were desks, children, chairs, and visitors to circumvent. In addition, the children were observant and conscious of each other's patterns. They were able to pick out the classmates who had done something unusual and to name the specific parts of the body influencing the movement ("She's leading with her elbow"). They understood the quality of movement as well as its direction ("He goes up light and comes down heavy"). They were aided by a teacher who recognized the individual quality and rhythm of each child's actions and who made constructive comments when necessary. Movement classes of this kind provide the child with new avenues of communication and the chance to learn as much by moving as by seeing, hearing, and talking.

As with other parts of the curriculum, teachers have capitalized on a crucial asset. They have attempted to make the most of the zest for life which children express in their games, in the way they balance on a curb on their way to school, and in the way they run in a series of rhythmic leaps from one corner of the playground to another.

We know that babies first learn through physical sensations and movements as they reach for things, manipulate objects, and test shapes with mouth, hands, feet, and any other part of the body that happens to make contact with the object. While many parents and psychologists alike recognize the importance of this early experimentation, teachers have not always realized that the connection between movement and learning continues as the child grows older. A number of educators in both England and the United States now feel that a degree of competence in physical skills is essential to learning to read and write. Basic movement activities that involve understanding one's position in space, following a sequence, hearing rhythmic patterns, noting differences and similarities, and expressing ideas and feelings are all related to other forms of learning.

There are many ways to aid the child's experimentation. We have described the simplest space available—a classroom with desks pushed to the wall—and many schools have substantial halls that they can use for a number of purposes. In this setting, many types of apparatus exist which enhance the children's experience. At an infant school in London, we watched a class use an apparatus, set up in the hall, which was simple and efficient. Small stepladders were connected to a horizontal ladder that the children could climb up and then crawl across. Climbing frames and bars for swinging were pulled out from the walls, and boards to walk and balance on were set up a few inches from the ground. What struck us most was a series of four plastic hoops, about three feet in diameter, which were set up on one side of the room. Each hoop was supported by two lightweight wire frames which held it either perpendicular or parallel to the floor. The hoops could be put in different brackets on the stands, encouraging the children to approach them in many different ways, and the children changed the heights and positions of the hoops frequently during the session.

The teacher asked them to "find your own way" of

going through, under, or around the hoops. Some children did a series of running movements, jumping through the hoops; others approached them from a low position, raising their bodies from the floor just enough to slip through and over the plastic in a snakelike, flowing movement. No two children used them in the same way. The child who first tried a quick, high method might take the teacher's suggestion to "try a smooth, slow way next time." When the positions of the hoops changed, so did the children's methods.

What we saw here was a startlingly simple but subtle use of ordinary apparatus. As these infants crawled over one hoop and under the next, they were learning what it means to go *through, over, under,* or *around* an object. They also encountered the words *above* and *below.* They were learning through the action of their own bodies. In this work, the teacher's choice of words is very important: "I liked the way you slipped under that first hoop, Jane."

The apparatus in this case gave the children an added dimension to explore physically. A child can use his body in space with no aids, and he can expand the possibilities with imaginative equipment.

This inventive use of equipment is repeated in many schools where the children have access to climbing ropes, large ladders mounted on the walls, balancing boards, and stools to vault over. Designers of this flexible equipment have been imaginative, and many different items are available for the schools. If a visitor enters a class where the children are using this equipment, he is struck by the independence exhibited by the children; by the way each child seems to know the limits of his body ("I climbed halfway up the rope today, Miss, and that was far enough").

The teacher in the middle of this activity gives the

children some direction. He may urge them to explore different equipment or suggest a new method of climbing a rope. As with much of the work that has gone on in the classroom, there is little need for commands. The children are purposeful. They know their own minds; they rest when they are tired and then go on to something else.

The development of basic skills is an outgrowth of the teachers' belief that the children learn a great deal from a deeper understanding of their own bodies and how they function. They may do this in a creative movement class with no equipment or in a school hall with apparatus. They may also do it on the playground.

Some schools have added large, grassy mounds, barrels, and boards to the more traditional outdoor climbing frames and slides. In city schools, where the paved playground is still the rule, many staffs have tried to acquire all sorts of objects to cluster in parts of the playground—wooden packing crates and oversize wooden building blocks abound. Good teachers try to give the children the opportunity to combine play, fantasy, and physical exercise.

Games are of the children's own choosing, and many of them are not competitive. There is seldom coercion on the part of the teachers to exclude competition; it is simply left to the children to introduce it in a natural way. Sometimes junior-school boys will organize a friendly though avidly played game of soccer. For other children, skipping rope, running a race, or beginning a game of dodge ball with complicated rules can become highly competitive for a while if the need arises. In some junior schools, however, highly competitive sports continue to the exclusion of all else. In at least two cases which we observed, new head teachers facing this situation banned all competitive sports. Although this seems a harsh countermeasure, these schools may well be able to return to a more natural situation in time.

A school in a poor London neighborhood has found that movement aspects of physical education can be more than a means of self-expression and an aid to learning. It can be therapeutic. On our visits to the school, we have seen the hall given over to a group of infants who, in the words of the head, "need to run, to make noise, and to move freely." A teacher gave them a variety of things to work and play with, including large toys the children could ride on, small climbing frames, and tubs for sand and water play. When this group was in the hall, they did not behave wildly although they were free to run and shout—and to race across the floor on top of a wooden truck with a roar of motors and the toot of horns. Their movements were expansive and full of great energy. They were carefully supervised, but not directed. They had a chance to explore the space of the hall and to work off energy until they felt ready to go back to their classrooms and profit from the activities available to them there. At the same time, this allowed their teachers to devote needed time to other children. This was a case where the staff had jointly found the means to deal with the special needs of a small group of children.

In another London school we saw a similar group of infant-school children suffer a different fate. There, the teachers felt that to cure them of their problems they needed a remedial class, but what they succeeded in establishing was in no sense remedial; it was a class in discipline. We witnessed eight fidgeting children forced to sit rigidly in their seats and told to "Listen to me!" by a teacher who had very little to say. Similar "special" classes can be found in some American schools, set up for children who need, among many other things, active, purposeful play and movement to help them toward further learning. The kind of work going on in the first school provides needed lessons for many teachers in the United States as well as in England.

The children who played freely in the hall of the first London school were interacting constantly with each other and with the woman who participated actively in their play. Human relationships were developing among a group of children who needed them vitally.

Movement which is used for a multitude of ends in English primary schools has become an integral part of life in many classrooms. In Bristol, we saw an excellent example of how movement can help teach specific skills when we watched a class of six- and seven-year-olds doing "math in the hall." The floor of this hall was made of linoleum tiles whose mathematical uses were soon apparent.

The teacher gave the children varied lengths of clothesline and asked them to enclose, for example, "a shape of twenty." A child might bend his rope around two rows of ten squares, or four rows of five squares, in both cases forming a rectangle. Or he might choose an entirely different method, ending up with an L-shaped enclosure of twenty tiles. Two children joined their ropes together and painstakingly discovered how many tiles could be enclosed within their ropes. The teacher moved from one group to another, making suggestions and watching as the children attacked the problems. The children profited from dealing with numbers in this way. Their whole bodies were involved in this large-scale work as they knelt on the floor to straighten a rope, or paced out the number of squares, or walked along the perimeters of their shapes, counting carefully.

This kind of movement, combined with more traditional school tasks, is also informative about the children's capabilities and drawbacks in other areas. The head and another teacher in this school had once despaired of a boy who was unable to read. They could not discover the source of his problem. One day, during a session of math in the hall, the head asked the child to count the squares in his shape and realized, while watching him, that he was unable to count from left to right. This was the basic obstacle which had kept him from reading—an inability to follow words and letters in the usual way. Teachers in this school now make it standard practice to ask the children to "count as if you were reading." They reinforce, through physical movement, a skill which is basic to being able to read. At the same time, the observant teacher can pick out the child who has troubles in this area and deal with them before he has a chance to fail.

A child who has the opportunity to explore spaces, ideas, forms, and patterns in these many ways with his body can learn a great deal about the world around him. He is growing in the type of awareness emphasized by Molly Brearley, principal of the Froebel Institute College of Education, when she wrote:

> Do we give the rich, sensory experience of color, shape, sound, smell and touch which will enable children to interpret the poetry, the stories, and the music . . . ? They cannot be creative without this basic experience.[9]

The child who is given this opportunity communicates a great deal about himself to the teacher. The boy who has been unable to relate to the teacher in the classroom may suddenly reveal an unusual capacity for bodily expression which will help the teacher to draw him out in other areas.

In all forms of movement—almost more than in any

other subject in the curriculum—it is vitally important to stay away from a strict method of teaching. Although there are universal concepts and ideas which teachers wish to communicate to their children, there can be no dogma which rules the teaching of movement. Most of the best teachers experiment with a variety of techniques. Some days their own voices are all that is needed to get the class going. They may use a small drum, a tambourine, or a simple Carl Orff xylophone to give rhythmic quality to the class. On other occasions, teachers use records or tapes which they feel fit the need of that day.

The most successful classes are those in which the teacher takes an active role, moving with the children and suggesting new directions and ideas with words as well as with his own body. Ian's teacher, who led the class in exploring calypso rhythms (discussed in Chapter One), is a fine example of how the teacher's involvement encourages the children to make the most of their own imagination and abilities as well as to enjoy the feeling of being physically alive. Those with little idea of where to begin would watch their teacher's interpretation, imitate it for a minute, and then find their own individual movements, looking only occasionally to their teacher for guidance.

In Ian's class, the development of the concept of rhythm was not limited to the movement class but was reinforced by other work in the classroom. Earlier in the year, we had listened to the class accompany similar music from a record player with drums they had made. They covered ordinary flower pots with six to eight layers of papier mâché and played the drums like bongos. In the fall, there had been a few children unable to follow the beat, but when we watched them in movement a few months later, we could see that the reinforcement of rhythm had paid off in both areas. The children moved with the music, in itself a hard task for some infant-school children, and were able, within that framework, to explore different ways of interpreting rhythmic patterns.

This teacher had a great deal of experience in both music and dance and was able to combine the two very successfully without depending on the record player as the sole source of inspiration. She was also able to make use of dramatic situations with her own class and others in the school. Obviously, not every teacher possesses this ability and for those who know little about the teaching of movement, the subject as a whole presents many difficulties. There is a danger that some teachers will never go beyond the use of a record, letting the music run the class instead of provoking the children to movement with original ideas, words, or simply, silence.

The B.B.C., the government-owned radio and television network, produces a great number of programs for schools, and one of them is a movement class for infants. For the teacher with little experience, these programs provide immediate help and good ideas for further exploration. But some teachers treat them as a crutch. We witnessed classes where teachers turned on the radio, tuned in the program, and stood to the side of the hall while the children followed the broadcast. The programs are of varying quality, but many good teachers feel the radio tells the children to accomplish tasks that are far too specific. Watching one class that had been told to "jump like a rabbit," we noted an unusual similarity between the movements of the children. We also felt that no rabbit had ever jumped in the manner described by the broadcaster. Here was a case where the children would have benefited more if the teacher had asked them to observe the school's pet rabbit and then interpret his hopping and running with their own bodies.

There is a definite need in movement classes to stay away from gadgets and methods that formalize any of the activities. Rudolph Laban highlighted this in relation to the use of music and argued that music should be adaptable to the movements of the individual, not vice versa.[10]

In many English primary schools much more complex work with music and movement could be developed. Diana Jordan suggested many possibilities in this area. The child, using the simple percussive instruments that are seen in many schools, could become a composer of music for dance, or of dance for music. Some of this work is under way, but many opportunities are missed. In the West Riding of Yorkshire, we watched another talented teacher conduct a marvelous movement class where juniors were working with partners. Each child responded to the movement of his partner in a variety of ways, and their teacher was very involved in their work. Later we watched the same woman lead her class in a rousing half-hour of song, greatly enjoyed by the children who rocked and tapped their feet as they sang. Yet they were seated solidly in chairs. We wished their enthusiasm for singing, expressed in their bodies, had been given freer rein through more expansive movement.

In isolated schools we have seen examples of movement classes which act as the core and focus for a variety of other experiences, particularly the need to create unity between an individual's inner life and the world around him. Again, this was one of Laban's concerns. He felt that man engaged in two kinds of thought: movement thinking and word thinking. He believed that these two processes had lost touch with one another and that, in many cases, men had forgotten how to think in terms of movement. He wrote:

> Movement-thinking could be considered as a gathering of impressions of happenings in one's mind, for which nomenclature is lacking. This does not, as thinking in words does, serve orientation in the external world, but rather it perfects man's orientation in his inner world in which impulses continually surge and seek an outlet in doing, acting, and dancing.[11]

At a school near Oxford we witnessed a movement class run by the head of the school which achieved the type of unity which Laban emphasized. The class was made up of lower juniors, eight- and nine-year-olds, including by chance a large number of slow learners who were badly in need of help with language development. The head, working with their teacher, hoped to boost their facility for words through movement.

After a few exercises to help the children relax, the head teacher asked if they remembered the way the pear tree outside their classroom window had moved in the wind on the preceding day. The children described the tree's motion in the strong fall wind and then spread out across the floor to show him in movements how the tree had bent and swayed wildly. In the background, the sound of the head teacher's tambourine caught their rhythm and pushed them forward with a gusting, rattling sound. The children then talked about the falling leaves and interpreted them in movements that were more delicate, floating, and swirling. Those of us who were watching felt that these children had captured a piece of the world around them.

This half-hour of movement took place at the beginning of the morning. The teacher then took his class to a nearby park, where they looked for evidence of motion in the woods, talked at length about what they saw, and made some fairly accurate observations about the way things in nature respond to the wind.

When they returned to the classroom, the children and their teacher reviewed and expanded some of the words and descriptive phrases which had come out of the morning's experience. Eventually, many people in the class were writing short poems, full of sharp imagery evoking the movements we had seen them use in the hall.

Clearly, this was more than a lesson in language development. Many children made important discoveries about the use of words and learned that language could be another means of expressing themselves. As each child tossed his body across the floor, blown by his imaginary wind, we could read in his movements something of himself; how he felt about the pear tree outside his classroom, the fall day, and his own body. This, which Laban often called "movement-thinking," certainly revealed some of the child's inner thoughts and feelings. Aided by the visit to the park, they had been able to work in another medium of expression: the spoken and written word, an area which was difficult for many of these children. Through movement they had been better able to cope with language. They had achieved unity between movement-thinking and word-thinking—between the inner and the outer word. Each child had learned quite a bit about his powers of self-expression, and much of his being had been thrown into the efforts of the morning.

Movement can add special qualities to the life of a school. Classes like this do not occur in every primary school, but they are not unique. When they do take place, these sessions reveal the acceptance by teachers of the fact that the child learns by using his body as much as in any other way and that it is essential to draw movement into the curriculum.

CHAPTER TEN

The Use of Space

BRITISH PRIMARY SCHOOLS, like their counterparts in America, vary enormously in quality and design. Some are massive Victorian monuments to education, built to last forever; some are tiny village schools that take in expansive views of the countryside; others are modern structures full of sunlight, and a few are examples of inspired design. Whether the school is in a suburban area or a rundown neighborhood with a rapidly shifting population, the visitor can learn a great deal about the quality of life in the school by observing the ways in which teachers and children use the building. The imaginative use of space, in the classroom and throughout the school, is an exciting aspect of primary education in England, as well as an ingredient essential to the achievement of fine work.

The philosophy of a school is often reflected in the degree of mobility granted to the child. In a great number of good schools, he is not confined to a specific desk or classroom throughout the day. His teacher may well expect him to move around the room or the school, attending to work in progress. Some teachers and educators recognize that the working needs of children are no different from those of adults. That is, different modes of work require different working spaces. The child needs a variety of areas in which to pursue painting, writing, drama, woodwork, mathematics, pottery, and so forth. The school which can provide this diversity in its surroundings can greatly enhance the child's learning conditions.

The classroom itself is indicative of the school's response to the children. As we have described earlier, the infant class makes great use of small tables and chairs in groups. In old schools, lacking new equipment, these "tables" may be four old desks pushed together; elsewhere, four or five children often share a round table. As the children sit in groups, engaged in similar projects or different tasks, they are free to talk and discuss the work at hand. In fact, both the grouping of desks and the round tables encourage worthwhile discussion, focusing inward on the small group. Teachers know that children learn from one another, and the arrangement of the schoolroom furniture promotes this interaction.

In both infant and junior classes, the room is often divided into distinct working spaces, or bays, by partitions made of the best available material: sometimes heavy cardboard, a bookcase on wheels, a cabinet, or a screen. In many cases, these partitions are temporary and the teacher can easily change them. In one corner, there may be a table for displays of different sorts. One week the teacher may set up an exhibit of pottery with some pieces from the local museum; another week might find the table covered with a project recently finished by the children.

The display area contrasts with the groups of tables

for general work and with other corners set up for specific purposes. The library corner is one such space, an area set apart for quiet reading. It is often the most pleasant and comfortable place in the classroom and includes small, stuffed armchairs, rocking chairs, and a rug (an addition which makes a great difference.) Attractive displays of books line the shelves and tables. The corner is usually divided from the rest of the room, and one or two children often sit there to read quietly to themselves or each other.

In infant classrooms, an enclosed space encourages quiet responses from the children. They know that there are other areas of the room where they can make noise. An open end of the room is used for water and sand play (each in its own plastic trough). Here, the floor is covered with a material which can easily withstand spills, and the children can scoop sand or pour water from one container to another without having to worry about making a mess. If they do spill, equipment is handy for them to clean it up. There may also be large easels nearby where the children can paint, and a big table for other messy work.

Teachers in many infant schools, both old and new, feel that their classrooms are never big enough for the forty children who so often occupy them. Some of these schools have expanded to include the outdoors as part of the classroom space. The architects of new schools often design an outdoor play area for groups of classrooms. Doors open out onto these paved surfaces, and in good weather in the spring, fall, and summer terms, the children move water tubs, easels, and building blocks outside. They work in full view of the teacher, who can glance outside now and then to watch their progress.

Woodwork is also an ideal outdoor activity for both

infants and juniors. Out on the paved area or on the grass, the children are free to bang away without disturbing the rest of the class. The tools for the infants are small and simple: tiny saws, hammers, screwdrivers, and vises. These are not toys, but well-made, usable tools. The children know they must be careful, and they are. The child who saws away vigorously at a future airplane gains practice in small motor skills and feels the pleasure of involving his whole body in the work. In this case, the outdoor space is a great asset.

A few infant schools are now lucky enough to have an aide who serves a couple of classrooms. She can work outside with the children, relieving some of the congestion in the classroom. This gives the teacher the chance to continue work indoors with smaller groups of children.

Some old schools, especially those in urban areas which are starved for space, have added enclosed outdoor working areas to the classroom. Here the children work at large, messy activities. Other schools have extended a plastic roof over a portion of the playground adjoining the building. Unless it is bitterly cold, the children can go out and work there (an added advantage for those who have little place to play outside school). In any case, the purpose is usually to expand the existing teaching space. What goes on outside is intrinsically related to what takes place in the classroom.

All of these different spaces imply a recognition, on the part of the school, that the primary child needs to move, to make noise, to talk. He needs room to build things, to take things apart; room to sit quietly, to think, to engage in fantasy play and drama. Spaces for role playing and games are just as important as the areas set aside for writing, math, or quiet reading.

The intelligent use of flexible spaces in the classroom

can stimulate the child's interest in different activities. In addition to the ingenious arrangement of furniture, there is the added stimulus of work displayed on the walls of the room. Some schools have done away with the bulletin boards so common to English and American classrooms and have covered their walls with extensive amounts of corkboard or corrugated paper. The entire wall surfaces are open to display paintings, poems, stories, and art work made of three-dimensional materials. These displays are changed constantly throughout the year and are different from one part of the room to the next.

Junior classrooms seem to suffer more from lack of space than do infants'. In part, this is because the children are bigger, and the work that they undertake often requires more room. For example, a group of children in one school made a series of large mobiles depicting the development of space flight from Icarus to Apollo 12. There were a number of boys at work on this project, and they needed a great deal of space to spread out their materials, the books they were reading, and the mathematical calculations they had made. The English teacher who works with thirty-five to forty junior-age children, in a classroom overflowing with students and equipment, faces a predicament that is familiar to many an American teacher. Both wonder how they will be able to provide nearly forty children, some of them approaching adolescence, with sufficient space to pursue a number of different activities.

Some teachers, in England and in the United States, feel that the only way to deal with this issue is to sit the children at their desks and have them work as a group. Others, in both countries, have found that this is not always fair to the children and that there are ways to open up even the smallest room. Many English teachers have rid themselves of the old belief that each child must have a place to sit and a desk in which to store his books, pencils, and notebooks. They realize that, with some children standing in a corner painting, a few down the corridor practicing the recorder, two out on the playground involved in some complicated measurement, a few in the library, there is little need to provide a seat for each child. They cut down on the number of chairs and push existing desks together. This opens up the room and expands the working area.

Many teachers at first react negatively to the removal of furniture. Where, they may ask, do the children sit if the teacher wants to call them all together as a group? And where do the children keep their work, if not in their own desks?

The children sit on the floor or on tables if there is no other place to sit. This is seldom a problem. When the school comes into the hall for an assembly, they naturally use the floor, for chairs would be a hindrance in a room that serves so many purposes. The removal of chairs and desks does not mean that the teacher never calls the children together in the classsroom—far from it. Most classes, working in a free manner, come together a number of times during the day, apart from the numerous occasions when the teacher calls a momentary halt in order to point out the work of one group, to throw in new ideas, or simply to ask a question or make an announcement.

The British teacher's answer to the second question would be to affirm the child's need for a place to keep his things. A number of simple arrangements have been made, the most successful being a drawer for each child set into the wall or mounted in a movable cart. These drawers, made of light plastic, are about twelve inches wide, eighteen inches long, and three or four inches high, and are often removable. If a child needs his books or pencils, he can take the drawer out of the wall and carry it with him. Needless to say, the contents of the drawer are his property, just as if he had a desk of his own.

In the late fall, we asked an experienced infant teacher whether the child of five, on his entry to school, needs to claim a chair or a specific place in the room in order to feel secure. She felt, as do many other teachers in England, that this was not necessary. She pointed out that in her classroom, the children were told that the *whole room* belonged to them. Whether it was the math apparatus, the table in the corner, the rocking chair, or the pet guinea pig, each new child soon learned that he shared ownership with the other members of the class, and thus did not feel the need to guard a special corner of the room for himself.

Many children in England find themselves in classrooms which belong to them. This feeling of sharing is enhanced by the school's attitude toward time. In schools where there is no fixed timetable, and where the children often choose the time at which to work on a specific task, there is no need to fight for a place in the home corner or wait around to be next with tie dying. The child knows that he can work there later in the day, or the next day if he wants to, and that the teacher will do his best to give each child a fair share of his classroom's activities.

This is certainly very different from the atmosphere that overwhelms many American classrooms. There the child often struggles to be first in line or to leave the class first at the end of the day. He fights for a place near the teacher or competes with his neighbor to reach the head of the class. If classrooms belonged to the children, if each child shared equally in learning, and worked at his own rate, perhaps the intense struggle to be "first" would not be necessary, and children would no longer attempt to get what they want, regardless of others. The sharing of experiences, spaces, and materials in English classrooms leads to attitudes of cooperation and caring.

There is another, more crucial, implication of the English attitude mentioned here. In a classroom where the books, the class pet, the reading and math corners, and so on, are the property of each child in the class—where the school itself is a domain shared by all the students—the child is more likely to feel that learning also belongs to him. This is an issue raised in the American context by George Dennison in his book *The Lives of Children* and by John Holt in a review of that book. Holt was speaking of American students, from the youngest to those of college age, when he wrote:

> . . . their schools and teachers have never told them, never encouraged or even allowed them to think, that high culture, all those poems, novels, Shakespeare plays, etc. belonged or might belong to them, that they might claim it for their own, use it solely for their own purposes, for whatever joys and benefits they might get from it.[1]

Obviously, it takes more than moving the furniture and placing the school at the child's disposal to convince him that the world of learning belongs to him. It is our belief, nonetheless, that many English children have been started in school feeling that they can take part in learning and, furthermore, that learning is an enjoyable, interesting, and compelling experience. Opening the school to the child is a first step in the process of opening the child's mind to the world around him. An important lesson in trust is conveyed to the child when he is allowed to move about the class and the school with few restraints. This must, of course, be reinforced by respect for the child, belief in the interaction between child and teacher, and by the other concerns, mentioned previously, which bring these schools to life. No arrangement of a school, no matter how ingenious, can compensate for poor, unimaginative teaching.

In good schools, freedom of movement extends to the child's use of the entire building. This mobility arises from the school's eagerness to share information and ideas. Children often participate in activities taking place in other classrooms, while many teachers are involved in various forms of cooperative teaching. Both children and teachers profit from the chance to see what others are doing.

We saw a class of juniors experimenting with silk screening. They had never tried it before, and a small group was hard at work with their teacher in an attempt to find the best method of making a clean print. At that moment, the deputy head, who also had a class of junior-age children, walked in to borrow something, and stayed for ten minutes to watch. He was not at all worried about being away from his class. He returned with knowledge about an art form that was new to him and a determination to try it with his own group. This sharing of ideas leads naturally to a sharing of materials among children and teachers and to a feeling of cooperation throughout the school.

Good head teachers and their staffs consciously try to make their buildings conducive to participation and increased mobility. They may create centers in the school which draw children and teachers together. A display of children's work has this effect, as does a central exhibit with a unifying theme. Whether based on metal work, glass, Japanese art and Haiku, or the stages involved in weaving cloth from natural wool, the objects are sure to include a crosssection of items, combined with children's writing and art work. It is not uncommon to see a child seated in front of such an exhibit, making an accurate drawing of an old pewter teapot or any other object seen there.

Whatever the age of the building, an effort is made to use every inch of space available. Narrow tables are set up in the corridors of many schools (still leaving ample space for children) and contain everything from a model of an English village to complicated mathematics apparatus. The children use these hallways as part of their working space, not just as passageways from one area to another. In one school, the corridor often resounds with the soft, clear tones of the large xylophone which has its place against the wall. Now and then, a small group of children pass by, listen to a girl who is picking out notes, and go on to their classroom, humming the tune.

Children in many schools are trusted in their use of the building and the materials in and around the classrooms. Because of the individual nature of their work, they learn very early to value what someone else has done. The child who spent a whole week on his model of the Severn Bridge was engaged in work that he cared about very deeply, and his long hours of intense concentration enabled him to understand the feelings of another child who had devoted two or three days to writing an original poem.

We saw an example in one school of the deep trust which can develop between a teacher and his class in the use of space. The school encouraged a positive response from the children, as was evident in the way they cared for the building and responded in their work. In its hall the school had a raised platform which was almost never used. The staff decided to partition it off, leaving a large "window" looking in on the hall. This space became a library for the entire school. A few children also recognized that this indoor window was the perfect size and height for a puppet show. Without supervision, children from different classes and age groups met in their new library to talk about ideas for puppet plays or to read and write.

A teacher in this school had developed a particularly good relationship with his children. One morning, he played a piece of music about the sea in connection with some impressionistic writing the children were doing. Two girls came to him and asked if they could work with the music for a while. They disappeared toward the new library with the record and were away all morning and most of the afternoon. When they reappeared, they produced a long piece of creative writing inspired by the music. It was beautifully written and full of imaginative images and ideas. The teacher was thrilled with their work and glad he had let them spend the day alone, without interruption. The fact that these girls were supported by their teacher, and that spaces in the building were provided for them to work on a project by themselves, encouraged them to produce work of outstanding quality.

OPENING THE SCHOOL

In the attempt to use space imaginatively, large amounts of time and money have been spent renovating old buildings and creating new schools to suit changing educational ideas. About one-half of the children now in primary schools in England are in buildings constructed before the First World War. [2] These massive structures contain cramped spaces, and present English teachers with many frustrating problems. Sometimes the head and his staff seem to give up on the building and bide their time while waiting for a new one.

In some old buildings, however, teachers are determined to alter the school and some ingenious adaptation takes place. One reason for the repeated success of renovations to old buildings is that the changes spring from the immediate needs of teachers and children. The alterations to the school described in Chapter Six are a good example; the teachers' scheme for alterations grew directly from the problems of day to day work. As is so often the case with old buildings, much of the effort at construction seemed to have focused on the area from floor to ceiling, while the classrooms themselves suffered from lack of floor space. The antidote devised by the staff included tearing down walls and opening the classrooms out onto the playground. Plastic roofs covered new outdoor play spaces, sinks were installed in the classrooms, two or three rooms were combined to form one large working space. Fortunately, this school was lucky to have the support of the local education authority; as an Educational Priority Area, it was entitled to extra money which was used to improve the school and hire additional part-time staff.

Changes of this sort seem simple enough on paper, but in fact they imply radical shifts in educational practice. This particular group of teachers changed their classrooms because they wanted to teach differently. They were prepared to combine their classes and put in the large amounts of extra time and effort required to work out the day to day organization of the work. There were other very good teachers in the building who were not ready to take this step. It is important to note that they were not forced to do so. Their colleagues respected their feelings on this matter, realizing that teachers have to work in the ways which seem most natural to them.

This same school, when renovated, provided an outstanding example of a building which was entirely open to the children. The corridors were full of children painting, talking, or going from one class to another. Mothers came in and out to help with special projects or to listen to the children read. On the rare occasions when the head teacher was in her office, she never closed the door. Children often came to her to show her their finished work and would stay to talk. The staff room was open to the children, and one or two were usually grouped next to a teacher for a chat during the morning break.

The school was also interesting because it defied most urban American attitudes toward the poor as well as the practices associated with these attitudes. These children, many of them West Indians, all from impoverished backgrounds, were not very different from their counterparts in the first and second grades of an American city school. They suffered from broken homes, lack of food and clothing, and many other disadvantages which are familiar to urban dwellers in the United States. Yet the school did not force them to line up outside the building or sit in regimented rows. The staff treated them as individuals and trusted them completely. Vandalism to the building declined radically as they were allowed to use it as their own, and the children made tremendous strides in learning. This school illustrated the many ways in which ingenious use of the building implies far-reaching educational goals and practice.

In Oxfordshire we saw another case of renovation in which space was used in other ways. The school building itself was new, but the town's population had grown suddenly. The school was forced to place a group of young juniors (seven-, eight-, and nine-year-olds) in an older, detached structure. There were three classrooms in the unit; the teachers decided to take off the doors—but to retain the partitions. The coat room, an area outside the classrooms, became a light, comfortable library. The oversized bathroom was changed into a working area for activities such as tie dying, painting, and woodwork.

While the infant teachers in the urban school described above felt they could share three groups of children between them, this unit for juniors worked out a different scheme. The children and teachers moved easily from one room to another, but the main activities of each class were carried on separately from the other two groups. However, the children from all three classes met in the art room and in the small library. If one group was engaged in a special activity that interested children from other classes, the latter would be free to join in. A student teacher, working in this building, drew children out of all three classes for a special project in prehistory. Ideas and projects flowed from one room to the next, and the three teachers were pleased with the balance they had achieved between an open situation and a closed one.

The success of this scheme lay in its adaptability. It allowed for changes in staff. If a new group of teachers were to teach in this building, the structure was such that they could choose to run separate classes, to combine all the groups for part of the time, or to work cooperatively for most of the day. Spaces which allow for differences in personal preference are often the most successful.

It is evident that tearing down the walls involves the intricate construction of new learning patterns. This is most apparent in some of the schools which have been built during the last twenty years, particularly those which are known as "open plan" schools. The new schools are worth discussion because they pose a number of difficult problems to teachers, yet contain obvious advantages over the older, more cramped buildings:

> We have seen ourselves that outstanding primary school buildings can support teachers in their use of modern methods, raise the standard of children's behavior and change their attitude to school, and win the enthusiasm of parents.[3]

New buildings have veered sharply away from the old concept of schools in which boxlike classrooms proceeded in orderly rows off the two sides of a long corridor. This design no longer fits the needs of modern primary education, and it also wastes valuable space. Plowden reported that only 40 per cent of the floor space in old buildings was used for teaching.[4]

The Plowden Report described some of the general developments which have taken place in school building since the 1950's:

> Much more compact plans were designed in which the total floor area was reduced by rather more than a third, although the amount of teaching space increased. . . . Buildings became more informal and domestic in character and likely to foster friendly, personal relationships.[5]

Modern schools represent many of the more interesting, yet economical, developments in British architecture. In many cases, the architects have provided children and teachers not only with more space, but with space which is imaginative and adaptable; with classrooms which are no longer isolated units, but integrally attached to the rest of the school. The schools are cheaper to construct, and contain more light, better equipment, and greater flexibility.

Still, many problems accompany these new structures. The architects of these ultramodern plans are sometimes more concerned with creating a monument to themselves than with designing a structure suited to the needs of the community.

Obviously, the success of a new design ultimately depends on the teachers who inherit the school. In areas where education has made tremendous strides over the last twenty years, there are fewer problems. One can usually find large numbers of staff who are eager to work with a new design, and who are experienced enough to deal with the educational philosophy implied by a new building. There are, however, many regions of England where primary education is just beginning to change, and it is these counties which have initial difficulties with schools that are more modern than the teaching within them.

Not all new buildings are radically designed. We have seen some extremely successful new schools which have combined new ideas with the working features of older buildings. One particularly good example is a school in Leicestershire where the junior area was designed as a separate block from the infants' (although attached to that building and under the same headship). To get to the junior area, one walked through the hall, into the wide entry used as a library, and down a few steps into a large working space. This area, equipped with long tables, was used for woodwork, painting, and any other activity requiring a great deal of space. Four junior classrooms radiated from this open area, which was used jointly by children from all the junior groups. The working space led naturally to the spread of ideas from one class to the next and to collaboration on different projects.

The extension of this type of design is the "open plan" school. These schools can be any size, from the village school for fifty children to the larger buildings designed for three hundred pupils. As the name implies, the schools are open. There is little attempt to distinguish one classroom from another. The whole building is used for teaching and learning in a variety of ways at once. The combination of a successful open plan and teachers who are competent to handle it is a joy to see.

Plowden's description of one of the first open plan schools illustrates the positive aspects of a school which is carefully designed:

> . . . the architects had observed a new relationship between teachers and children and a blurring of division between one subject and another, between theoretical and practical work and between one lesson period and the next. The "teaching area" was conceived as the whole school environment, rather than as a series of individual rooms. . . . "School" includes the buildings, garden, play area and games space. Outside and inside provide an integrated learning environment. Inside, there are small working areas each with a degree of privacy and a character of its own, opening onto a larger space sufficiently uncluttered to allow children to climb and jump, dance and engage in drama. Among the small working spaces is a sitting room, a library, two workshops with water available, a kitchen and three group study spaces.[6]

We were fortunate to see the school described here, and felt that the environment created by the unity of the school with the grounds was ideal for children. The pupils, ages five to eleven, saw little difference between the rolling, hilly ground outside and the open, light areas within the school. Two girls, who were eager to show us around, felt that the important things to see were the little stream full of flowers in front of the school; the hedgerow in back, where, said one of the girls, "I counted and identified fourteen different kinds of plants growing"; and the lovely, natural hill which was a wonderful place to sit and sketch (as two girls were doing). They were anxious as well to show us the library, inside, and the home corner. The architect had designed a nook long enough to hold a large bed. Light yellow curtains ran from floor to ceiling, and children could pull them across, making a cave or a house out of the little alcove. When we peeked in, two girls had taken their chairs in behind the curtains and were sitting next to the bed, minding the "baby" who was sleeping there. This was not a stereotyped Wendy House, but a real home corner in a full sense.

This building was entirely open, although bays, screens, and nooks made a series of interesting small spaces. There were also two sliding doors, made of wood, which could be closed to make the school into two small classrooms and a hall. It was obvious that the architect of this building had a deep understanding of children. He had designed a structure full of variety, which was unified with the landscape outside and which gave the two teachers working there maximum flexibility. The building itself was very inexpensive and one of the best examples of what excellent design can do for the child in school.

Size does not always determine the success of an open plan school, although teachers we consulted in England generally felt that one hundred and fifty to two hundred pupils should be the maximum. Yet one of the more successful open plans we saw was used by over three hundred children of infant age. It was workable mainly because the staff was led by a dynamic head teacher and because the group believed wholeheartedly in the design. In addition, there were enough closed areas to provide maximum fluidity of teaching methods.

These schools provide innovative teachers with vast opportunities to work imaginatively with children. But they can pose many problems. In their own way, the inflexible open plans deny teachers and children the adaptability which seems an essential quality to good practice in primary schools, regardless of the design. When an additional misfortune occurs—a head teacher and a staff who do not understand their new open plan building—chaos results. One open plan school which we visited faced this predicament. Neither the head teacher nor her deputy believed in the idea of open planning, and they thwarted all reasonable attempts to use the building properly. The sound proofing was inadequate (or nonexistent) so that "quiet spaces" were just as noisy as the messy working areas. A few teachers were trying to run formal classes in spaces designed for movement and noise. It was a building full of problems, unhappy teachers, and nervous children.

Architects and educators must take care that an open plan building does not undo much of the exciting work that goes on in schools with a unified curriculum. A building that puts too much emphasis on the separation of art from academic work may encourage a division of subjects that no longer exists in the best English schools. To reimpose these barriers could be disastrous. Spaces must be inventive, but adaptable. They must lead to further integration of subject matter. The building should provide empty spaces without a purpose as well as areas for specified activities. The corner with no specific intent is often the one most effectively used by the children for projects of their own choosing.

These buildings, when well designed, lead naturally to cooperative teaching of all kinds and to a sharing of ideas among staff members. This positive aspect of open plan schools by no means demands specialization on the part of the teachers. Some, unfortunately, have interpreted it this way. The primary school is rarely the place for intense specialization; the children in England, as elsewhere, can find that experience in secondary school. The school must draw on the talents of the teacher—in art, drama, music, poetry, pottery—but not force him to stay with this subject throughout the day. He must be able to use his own talents throughout the school's curriculum. If he is isolated within a subject, he will see only one part of a child and miss out on that child's full development.

This is not an indictment of all open plan schools, but it does illustrate the need for more careful planning. In many cases, the architect never consults the future head teacher or his staff, even when the local authority knows who they will be. It is essential that teachers have a say in the design of buildings. English teachers have tremendous discretion in their classrooms, and they have proved, in many areas, that this has made a positive difference in the education of the children. The adaptations of old schools have shown that the teacher's ideas are often more practical than the grand schemes of the most well-meaning architects. The architects must listen to those who will work in the new structure.

There is one further development in the practice of opening up the schools which is often very exciting.

This is the attempt that some authorities make to integrate the school building with the surrounding environment. There is often a conscious effort to make the outdoor play spaces more unusual. Paved areas for games are joined to grassy fields. An inner courtyard in the school is filled with sand; another with water. Rather than bulldoze the field around a school, the builders may leave the original contours there for the children to explore. Gardens, with plants that are tended by the children, adjoin some schools. There are often rabbit hutches near the building, and a number of infant schools raise chickens (using the collecting and selling of eggs for some inventive mathematics).

As in America, most urban schools provide little or no play space for the children. But many city schools in England make an attempt to improve the little space they do have. A large nursery in Bristol, close to the railroad tracks, filled its playground with attractive and useful equipment. Huge barrels, rubber tires, rope swings, and climbing equipment of all sorts extended the possibilities for play.

A private nursery in London, a leader in nursery education for many years, provides its children with one of the most exciting and imaginative environments we saw in a year in England. The school has transformed an enormous artist's studio into what now might be called an open plan school, although the nursery was operating this way long before the term was coined.

The visitor enters a large room where about one-third of the forty children are working on a wide variety of activities, from painting and block building to riding rocking horses and experimenting with musical sounds. In a smaller adjoining room children are talking to a teacher at a table. This room is shut off from the bigger room a number of times during the day: when there is a creative movement class with music, which a small number of children join; before lunch, when one teacher reads a story to a group of children; after lunch when the youngest sleep there for an hour.

Both these rooms open onto a garden which has not changed much since it was originally landscaped for the owners of the studio in the 1920's. The garden is ideal for all sorts of exploration; it is enclosed on all sides, yet trees and varied contours give the illusion of space. At one end is a partially covered area for outdoor play in bad weather. The rest of the garden is open. Its center slopes down to a pit, where the children play all sorts of games or make mudpies. (There is a hose handy for this purpose.) The garden is full of unusual humps of land, bushes, flowers, rock formations, and natural growth of all kinds. All the climbing apparatus blends into the feeling of the garden. Needless to say, this space is used just as much for learning and play as the area inside. The children go in and out as they wish, and there is always a teacher outside to help with building schemes, settle disputes, observe, and talk. This school is an example of how an unusual plan, combined with teaching of the highest quality, contributes to the success of an exceptional school.

Schools which use space imaginatively can no longer be inward-looking. They have abandoned the idea that the walls of the classroom mark the boundaries of the child's learning. They now look beyond the walls of the school itself, and beyond the grounds, to consider the outside world. Teachers want their children to participate fully in firsthand experience and feel that there is a limit to the amount of firsthand material that can be brought into school. They also realize that the child has another life outside the building which is equally important to his growth. For schools which have opened themselves to learning more about children, the natural step beyond is to take the children out into the community.

CHAPTER ELEVEN

Outside the Classroom

ENVIRONMENTAL STUDIES is a newly coined term for an old English custom: using the outdoors. The English have long been known for their enjoyment of nature and their fondness of gardens and walking. Even city dwellers in England are great outdoors lovers—thanks to fewer cars and more trees than in America, and to numerous parks easily accessible to large numbers of people. English teachers who take their children outside the school are coordinating an existing appreciation for nature with a belief that a child's full development is not confined to the classroom. In some senses, the present encouragement in England for children to undertake extensive studies of their environment is only a change in degree. Nonetheless, this merging of an older philosophy with new ideas in teaching has led to work that is often unusual, rewarding, and stimulating to all concerned.

The environmental studies now in progress in some English primary schools vary from one area to another. Differences appear both in the type of study undertaken and the number of ways in which teachers and children choose to approach the subject at hand. Our inquiries suggest that most teachers in England think of the environment as anywhere outside the school and usually out-of-doors—not in buildings. While some of the work they encourage children to undertake centers on natural objects in natural settings, teachers also take advantage of the wealth of life and material available in the city streets, factories, and waterfronts.

In addition to the Englishman's love of nature, a number of more recent influences have encouraged an increase in studies that take place outdoors. One such influence is the emphasis placed on environmental problems by the mass media. In Britain as in the United States, concern is mounting over pollution, waste disposal, preservation of resources, and so on. Although felt throughout the country, this emphasis seems to have acted as only a mild encouragement to teachers to take groups into natural areas outside the school. More specific urging and advice has come from other quarters, notably from material devised for use in modern mathematics and science.

In England, the Nuffield Foundation has been in the forefront of curriculum development in math and science. Their Modern Mathematics Project material encourages contact with physical objects and quite naturally leads to work outside the school. Most of the suggestions for outdoors work in mathematics do not venture far afield. Measuring and estimating playground sizes, dealing with the heights of buildings, and counting and graphing all manner of things are common suggestions, likely to be possible in the widest range of schools. Nuffield Mathematics also advocates collection of natural materials for counting, weighing, and measuring. In addition, the teacher can employ some suggestions in Nuffield books to use the environment of his particular school to the fullest advantage. Once children become involved with conservation of numbers and with sets, they can begin to classify objects into sets and groups both inside and outside the classroom. The children can experiment with everything from varieties of leaves to buildings in the town. Encouragement to work with math outside the building is far more limited, however, than is advice and information on how to use the environment in studies of science.

In science as in mathematics, the Nuffield Foundation and Schools Council materials are those teachers encounter most often. Much of their emphasis is on outdoors work in a natural setting. In the *Nuffield Junior Science* series, which contains four teachers' texts on scientific work in junior schools, 65 per cent of the classroom examples point to specific uses of the environment outside the classroom as integral parts of the children's work.[1] The series makes concrete suggestions of valid areas of study. It also offers a multitude of approaches based on the needs and interests of individual children. The introductory chapter of the first *Teacher's Guide* proposes a broad definition of science, cast in the light of children's interests, concerns, and development.

The most recent Nuffield and Schools Council project, called *Science 5/13,* proposes scientific work for all the primary school years.[2] It also encourages use of the environment. In *Science 5/13,* which emphasizes more specific objectives for children than *Junior Science,* slightly over 60 per cent of the different aspects of the proposed units have to do with work outside the classroom. One entire unit, "Structures and Forces," leads children in and out of the classroom to observe manmade structures, make models, and explore their usefulness, design, and beauty through discussion and writing.

The science and mathematics units are extremely helpful aids to the instigation of projects, but they do not always provide the inexperienced teacher with the kinds of information he really needs. He soon finds that work taking place outside the school is unpredictable. Even the most carefully planned and teacher-directed study is likely to bring unexpected incidents. A child will discover something the teacher did not ask him to look for. A large group may not be able to identify an odd outcropping of rock, and the teacher will not have a ready answer himself. The carcass of a rabbit may be found in some tall grass, provoking a worthwhile discussion about predators despite the teacher's plan to deal with other subjects.

Taking a class on any but the most carefully prearranged expedition can be an alarming experience for a teacher. Small groups, short periods of time, or the assistance of a mother may not allay these concerns. Often a visit to another building—a museum or an art gallery—seems safer and more predictable. Of course, these visits can be very important, but teachers we spoke with in the course of the year argue convincingly that a natural, outdoors setting is often more valuable. It allows the children to be actively engaged in the materials at hand, not merely passive observers of museum cases. And such an honest approach often encourages the children to seek more answers on their own. They are lured toward books and other sources of information to answer questions they have felt a need to ask, not those posed by a teacher or a text.

Expert assistance is essential for the teacher who undertakes an environmental studies project. In England, a growing number of individuals provide this help. Some come from the local education authority as advisers and some are teachers in the schools. Lecturers in training colleges also offer advice on occasion to those who need it. While there are still only a limited number of people to give this help, it is invaluable when it does occur.

In England as in the United States, there appear to be two general approaches to environmental studies. The more traditional approach is directed largely by the teacher. He chooses a site. The group of children go there with prescribed tasks and assignments, having been told something about the area and what they should look for. On arrival, there is a bit of random examination and some discussion, then some children turn to drawing, some record with paper and pencil, and some collect samples shown on a list. They return to school to collate, write, rewrite, illustrate, and report.

A teacher who has worked this way for a while may sense some difficulties with this approach. The assigned tasks never seem to demand an equal amount of time. Some children throw themselves into their work while others wander off after dabbling in a project they agreed to undertake. The writers start writing too soon and observe very little. They are so anxious to finish their assignment about a particular pine tree that they fail to notice the moss growing on one side or the small hole at the base where an animal lives. A discipline problem may easily crop up with a few of the children, and the teacher, fearing the freedom of the outdoor space, may choose to limit or cancel further trips.

The second general approach is basically more child centered and attempts to deal with some of these difficulties. The teacher makes an effort to let the experience in the environment grow from the children's interests in many fields. This often necessitates working in smaller groups than the normal class size of thirty-five to forty. The group leaves the school for a site usually selected by the teacher, but the work accomplished there is never predictable. It will grow from the direct encounter of the child with the site itself. Yet, the work that the child carries out will not differ totally from what he would do in the more teacher-directed setting. The difference is one of degree and has to do with how the child settles upon a particular task or project and the encouragement he receives from his teacher.

Preparation for the field study takes a number of forms. If a child is sure of what he wants to look for, he may read something about the subject in advance. Others may note objects they think they will see. If the study requires special equipment such as traps, nets, shovels, sifters, large drawing pads, or any other specific items, children may build or collect whatever is needed. In all these cases, teachers and children will have done a substantial amount of talking ahead of time so that children preparing something do so of their own volition and with an understanding of the need for it. However, teachers skilled in this work sometimes like to take the children out of the school with very limited preparation. (The teacher would normally visit the site first to make sure it was worth investigation.) In this situation, the children arrive at the location with minds uncluttered by images from a confusing text. They are ready to talk, look, and think carefully about their surroundings.

Many English teachers encourage some note taking and sketching, but do not insist upon it. Skilled teachers prefer to encourage observation and discussion at the site. These teachers argue that children need to learn what appears important to them at the moment, to digest their experiences and put them to work in a manner that seems right to the child. Writing about an expedition is not always proof that the child's thinking has been sparked.

Teachers using a more child-centered approach to environmental studies are very conscious of the issue of writing about experiences. Many feel that we too often stifle the child's thoughts and feelings when we require him to write a report as soon as the field trip is completed. Good teachers argue that the child must come to the writing in his own way. If he invariably avoids writing, then a specific assignment may be helpful, but a child's work needs to be watched closely before making such a decision. Did the experience of an environmental studies trip become part of factual writing a few days later? Did it crop up in poetry or fiction? An affirmative answer is likely, for such experiences appear more often in writing of this sort than in a constant diet of reports.

This manner of work is strikingly successful in many schools. But it does demand skilled advice and leadership for the teacher who is just beginning to take the children out of the building. As he gains experience, he will develop his own techniques and skills in environmental studies. Many teachers speak of the need to start on a small scale. The school playground, the street outside, or a nearby abandoned lot may be ideal.

We accompanied a group of students from a training college in the city of York who had been asked to explore a street running alongside a primary school. These students had already investigated a site elsewhere in the city and had learned the value of an in-depth study of an area at their own level. They had enjoyed the previous site themselves, without relating it to work with children. Now they were to consider what children could get out of this street.

At first glance, the street offered little possibility for exploration. Rows of drab two-story Victorian houses, one identical to the next, stretched for blocks and blocks. Each had the standard low brick wall in front enclosing a plot for a tiny garden—a typical sight all over England. The gardens were largely untended or nonexistent.

After some careful observation, the students began to notice that the doors and doorknobs were all different. Each house had its own color and design, which was unique to the street. They found a number of interesting geometric shapes in the gates and were interested in the stone scrollwork around many windows. One student began to sketch a cluster of startling chimney pots on a roof. Another wrote about the silence of the street. Two women noticed a group of three-story houses which looked as though they had once housed a wealthier group of inhabitants. They began to speculate on the social history of the neighborhood.

In an hour, these students touched upon many things in the area that children would certainly find interesting. They had learned that a site which at first seems barren and lifeless may provide children with many ideas for work—if it is properly used. This is not to say that teachers should look for an intrinsically dull area, but that they should observe more closely those neighborhoods and vacant lots which one takes for granted. They may possess great potential for exciting work.

A film called "The Field Outside the School" illustrated how a junior class used a vacant lot for extended study. Made by a teacher at a primary school in Sheffield, the film was judged important enough to be shown repeatedly at a national exhibit in London marking the hundredth anniversary of the English universal education act. The field itself was not unusual—a vacant lot surrounded by housing developments and containing its share of trash thrown there by local residents. Yet its contents, shape, and topography were interesting enough to involve the class in an extended study over a period of four weeks.

Working in groups, the children identified thirty-four different varieties of wildflower. They made polystyrene contour maps of the field and the stream which ran through it. They tested the speed of the water by adding carefully measured amounts of vegetable dye and by timing the flow of match sticks. They ran soil tests and attempted a study of insect life within limited sections of the field. At the end of their study they had still not exhausted the possibilities for investigation. Detailed reports, stories, poems, paintings, and extensive mathematical projects resulted; they were all mounted and displayed for the rest of the school to examine and discuss.

The children involved in this project worked almost entirely in small groups. Although they decided on the tasks they wanted to undertake, they pursued specific jobs fairly steadily and did not spend much time wandering through the field looking for intriguing sights. Although frowned on by some teachers, we have seen that more casual examination of a chosen site can often provoke interesting talk and writing later—if a child sets out with the thought of observing and thinking about what is seen. This was the case for a nine-year-old girl living in a Yorkshire mining town, who wrote the following poem after a fairly private walk in the woods:

The leaves rustle in the wind
They move so gently that it
is lovely to hear them

they sound like Snowflakes which
is very soft. The branches of
the trees seem to be whispering
something in the wind. The top
of the tree moves more than
the bottom of the tree. The trunk
is hard and strong it never
blows away for it is very
strong and solid. The grass
sways in the wind and
is very long. There are about
six holes in one tree.

The girl's happiness on her walk and her growing ability to observe carefully, encouraged repeatedly by her teacher, are both evident in this story-poem.

In addition to concrete pieces such as this one, children write fantasies which reveal much about themselves. A girl living near an industrial city spent part of a morning ostensibly looking for ferns, but came back to write a story entitled "The Girl who Wanted to Live in the Woods." It read, ". . . and Mam hit Angela and she cried. And my Mam and Dad will be looking for me, but I am not going home and they was looking for six days." Her teacher was able to ask some careful questions and learn of a family problem that had been upsetting the girl for some time. Although her writing had nothing to do with ferns, it was a very important effort on her part, stemming from what she had seen and felt on an environmental studies trip. Fortunately, her teacher was able to give her help and comfort that might not otherwise have been offered.

Fantasies, however, are not always so deeply important. They are often written for fun, evoking elements of an experience that was intriguing to the writer. As part of a week's study in northern Wales, a group from a school near London visited a ruined castle which they mapped, explored, and studied at some length. Aside from the detailed work done on this castle, many stories were written. "Prison Tower" is by a ten-year-old boy.

I've been captured!
I get brought down the narrow
lightless staircase.
I get pushed and pulled about
as a dungeon door opens.
Thin boney hands reach up,
begging for food.
Am I to die like this, in this
dark, damp, frightening place and
die of suffocation?

This kind of writing, taken largely from the experience of viewing an exciting castle, is a natural offshoot of an environmental studies trip. The story was written by a boy who was not a casual visitor, but one who had explored and studied a castle in detail. Few schools, however, have the chance to take such an unusual trip. Most environmental studies have to take place on more familiar ground.

As we have noted earlier, a site near the school often offers many possibilities for exploration. The following pieces of writing illustrate the different way two children reacted to a trip to a park near their school:

IN THE PARK

Sun shines through the cold frosty branches like arms spread out from a long thin body. The sun is like shafts covering the branches. Colours orange red and yellow coming through spiny twigs. Branches with snow on them are like long strips of wood with snow on one side and green mossy bark on the other. Mist seemed to glide along past the spiny trees. The colourful figure of a woman and a child moves slowly into the swirling mist. All the colours seem to go blacker as they faded away.

217

THE PARK UNDER SNOW

The silhouetted trees like black
  lace.
Orange rays pour through the
  framework.
Becoming thicker as it fades away.
It does not reach the ground but dies
  away into the mist.
The sun is shining yellow
Staring through the black slim
  looking trees.
The mist devours up the trees and
  ground.

A school in a Yorkshire town also made good use of
an area close to the building. A class began to study the
site of a new housing development next to the school.
They examined the builders' work and explored the
excavations for signs of the area's past uses. This work
extended over a few days and led some of the class to
a greater interest in their town. They obtained a large
scale government map of the area, but were not satisfied with what it told them. They set out to make their
own map, and show not only every building but its
use as well. Although the final draft of this map was
made in the school, the work was done on site in the
town. The children also began a study of the agriculture
of the surrounding land, went on farm visits, and made
soil tests, land-use maps, graphs and stories. For some
members of the class, this was a consuming effort that
began in October and lasted until Christmas. Since the
class was run on an informal basis, those children who
wanted to devote a great deal of time to the project
could do so, while others turned to different work.

Needless to say, studies of the world outside the
school are not confined to rural or suburban areas. The
city child, more than his counterparts in small towns,
desperately needs both the time to play outside in

unconfined spaces and the opportunity to understand the complex and exciting variety of life on his block and in the city as a whole. Many urban schools in England strive to provide both of these experiences for the children, but there is a need for larger numbers to join in the attempt. Some cities, London in particular, have many parks, to which teachers take the children to play and to learn about the natural world.

In schools where teachers naturally share groups of children, part of a class can go out with their teacher to visit a site while the others join another class for part of the day. These visits may include work in the immediate vicinity of the school, a trip to a church, or a journey to the river to watch the ships, study the bridges, and examine both the manmade and natural objects that float in the water. Construction sites, open-air markets, subways, new high-rise buildings—all lead to work in mathematics, science, design, art, local history, studies of industry, and creative writing.

One lucky group of schools, located in the poorer areas of London, have gained the use of an abandoned secondary school in Kent (a county southeast of London). On a rotating basis, each school takes eighty children and some mothers out to the country every week, using the old school as a base while they explore fields, playgrounds, and places of historical interest. One class made friends in the neighborhood with a group of gypsy children, who have since joined them in outdoor projects. This opportunity is still too rare in most urban areas, but it has obvious benefits for the children as well as the teacher and the mothers, who enjoy the outings and learn a great deal about their children in the process.[3]

Experience of this kind, added to the progress made by many schools in environmental work, has convinced some teachers of the need to explore an entirely new setting, away from the school, the home, and the immediate neighborhood. "Let's not *read* about the sea," said a teacher in the midlands, "Let's go there, and see for ourselves."

Unfortunately, money is not always available for a week's trip to a residential center, although such camps are open in a number of areas, run by local education authorities, churches, and other groups. To fill the need for a base for one-day trips, a few L.E.A.'s have re-opened unused rural schools. These small one- or two-room buildings can be equipped with a few tables, chairs, running water, and some simple apparatus. Some grander schemes call for supplying the new center with scientific equipment and assigning a full-time specialist to aid with a wide range of projects undertaken there by the children. A few local authority officials with whom we talked envision a number of such centers set in distinctive, yet accessible, geographic areas throughout the region governed by their authority.

Whatever the site, however, the project that is done outside the school naturally leads back to the classroom. Just as there is preparation for a major environmental study, so there is the follow-up of further experiments, reading, writing, and artistic projects carried out in the school. Teachers and children need to think about what can be done in the classroom as a result of the work outside to make sure that the projects are carried to fruition.

The opportunity to work on environmental studies is neither a special privilege nor an area of study for the very good or the very bright alone. Environmental studies can be a great help to a child who appears to have little interest in school work and who may have become a behavior problem because of it. An example in an Oxfordshire school showed how this type of work inside the classroom can be of great benefit to many children.

Four boys, aged nine to eleven, were involved in this project. Their town, of five thousand people, had once had some importance as a railway depot. In recent years, service had declined and then been discontinued. About a year earlier, the rails had been taken up.

In the fall, the four boys, who had already expressed an interest in railroads, set out from the school to do some probing and excavation around the old station. After a good deal of work, they returned with a collection of metal pieces that ranged from heavy bolts to much larger, curiously shaped pieces. These objects caused a lot of discussion and speculation as to what they were. Teachers and families were consulted. Good drawings and photographs of engines, railroad cars, and station equipment were examined for clues.

These four boys had never shown much interest in schoolwork, although their school was a fine one, providing a good atmosphere and generally intriguing work. In encouraging their investigation of the railroad station, their teachers recognized that stringent demands and assignments would not help these boys to learn. They needed the excitement and adventure of exploration. Faced with this unusual experience, they responded with extensive talk and writing about what they had discovered at the station. They also did an extended project on railroads in general. They put their writing together in book form with illustrations. It was well covered and bound and provided an incentive to assemble an exhibit of their discoveries with the book as a guide.

Work which involves the children is also very helpful to the teacher. If the children are intrigued with their tasks—if they want to write about the railroad station—then the teacher is no longer faced with the problem of motivation. All his energies with these children can be devoted to encouraging a high degree of excellence in their work. When the children know their work will become a book which the rest of the school will see on display, they are usually determined to improve the writing, to spend more time on the art work, and to make the display as clear, handsome, and lively as possible.

Teachers who have had experience in this work in England point out that a project should stay with the original group of children. In the situation described here, the teacher had no intention of assigning the creation of the display to others. Nor did he think of doing it himself. The boys who started the study of railroads brought it to completion, largely on their own initiative.

The work at the railroad site also illustrates the success of work which is in the hands of a sensitive and skilled teacher who knows the material. In this case, the teacher had some knowledge of railroads and was able to help the boys overcome difficulties. This is particularly important in the case of a more natural site. Someone with a background in biology can add a great deal to the study of a stream, for instance, and a teacher beginning this kind of work should think of leading children toward environmental sites of which he has some knowledge. This caution does not mean that a teacher who feels unsure about most outdoor sites should never take children out of the school. A small group can often be successful with the expertise readily found in a few simple books. The honest teacher who will freely admit that he does not know an answer encourages children to seek solutions on their own.

A study of themselves and their environment can open children's minds in many ways. It gives them points of reference to compare and contrast other people's ways of life.

In addition, environmental studies gives children the chance to work and move about in natural settings, and this is probably its most important aspect. As man continues to overpopulate the world and destroy his surroundings, teachers have a tremendous obligation to bring children closer to the natural world. As they grow older, these children will not be interested in preserving a local forest or a city's river if they have never appreciated these areas in some special way—if they have not come to an understanding of the complex living communities that each supports. Environmental studies can continue the child's natural interest in the world of living things and can help him to understand that he is an essential part of this world—that his connections with plants and animals are very real and concrete. Hopefully, as ecological problems become more acute, environmental studies will become, as it has in a few schools, less a subject area and increasingly a distinct approach to much of primary education.

CHAPTER TWELVE

To Know the Child

THE GOOD TEACHER in any country seeks to know his children as individuals. Whether he only sees his pupils inside the classroom or has the chance to take them outside the school, he will hope to discover what his children are really like, what they care about, and how they feel in different situations. He is more concerned with who they are *now* than with what they should be like in five years. Yet even the most perceptive teacher still sees only a part of the child when experiences at home and in the neighborhood are totally remote and separate from life in school. In both England and America, some teachers have realized that the positive involvement of parents can lead to a fuller understanding of the child—and to better schooling for many children.

The role of the parents in English primary schools has a very poor history. Compared with the influence of parents in some communities in the United States, parents in England have little voice in educational affairs. They can complain individually or in force to their Member of Parliament, to members of the elected county or urban council, or to officials of their local education authority. They may be able to bring limited pressure to bear on the school through the often ineffectual "managers" of each school. But parents do not always wish to complain; they often seek to participate.

For many years, the highly selective system of English secondary education and the severely limited number of university places available created a situation in which teachers were often better educated than much of the rest of the population. Many teachers in England have seen themselves as the final custodians of the child's education, and they have tolerated little participation on the part of parents. Some feel that parental involvement threatens their professional status. Others have expressed a deep fear of the P.T.A., citing a number of suburban areas in America as examples. They feel that teachers in the United States have often abandoned creative, child-centered practices in favor of parents' wishes for a pressurized system in which the child's work, even at the ripe age of six, is clearly related to his progress toward college. English teachers are used to a substantial degree of freedom and believe that an overly directive P.T.A. would put restrictions on the innovations that this freedom has encouraged.

A more serious problem in both countries, however, is the disinterested parent who seldom pays much attention to his child's schooling. The common complaint of teachers in the United States and England is that the parent who never appears is the one the concerned teacher would really like to see. Many studies suggest that parental interest in the child's work can positively influence his learning, but far too few parents take the time needed to express such interest to the child.

While trying to lure disinterested parents, English schools also make attempts to ward off the parent who tries to pressure the school unduly. The schools are eager, however, to find ways in which interested parents can cooperate and participate in the child's learning. This is a very difficult line to tread, and we have seen only a few schools in England where parental involvement is purposeful and healthy, although a number of others try to achieve this goal. The Plowden Report notes at least one school where parents were not only included in numerous school gatherings while their children attended the school, but were invited to school functions two or three years before the children reached school age. The school hoped to be able to help the parents with problems and to keep informed about the children who would be arriving at the school in the future.[1] However, Plowden also makes a strong plea for a greater effort on the part of most schools to communicate with the parents. At this time, most of the developing relationships between parents and schools in England follow patterns that have been familiar in the United States for some time. Only a few exceptional instances are important to record here.

There are wonderful examples of English parents who donate their time and skills to the schools. Some have aided with environmental studies. Others have raised money for needed renovations. In some cases, fathers have built and designed libraries, cupboards, and whole additions. Mothers who enjoy cooking can be found in a number of infant schools helping with the preparation and baking of cookies, buns, and bread. Others help with reading or in other areas — music, drama, sewing, or pottery — where they may have special skills.

Many parents who help out in schools must ignore the National Union of Teachers' regulations on assistant helpers. The N.U.T. fears that untrained help in the classrooms will weaken the teacher's professional standing, an attitude which causes schools in England to miss out on a great deal of needed help. Schools which ignore this ruling find that the children gain from the chance to read aloud to an interested listener and profit from exposure to different people. It is certainly easier to use assistants in an informal setting. In a formal classroom dominated by the teacher, an assistant is often at a loss as to what he or she can do. In an informal setting, he has no choice. The children immediately involve him in the work at hand.

Some schools encourage forms of involvement which both bring the parents into the school and allow the children to go out into their communities. We visited an adopted "grandma" with a group of children from a junior school in Yorkshire. A different group from this class went to see this elderly lady every day during the break after lunch. They sometimes shopped for her and always filled her coal scuttle and put it beside the one fireplace that provided all her heat. The experience made the woman feel less lonely, and it was clearly valuable and enjoyable for everyone else. Nonetheless, this intelligent arrangement is a rarity in England just as it is in the United States.

Only occasionally do the parents and the community really share in the work of the children in school. Yet such sharing is the most natural way to bring the community and the school closer together and to allow the child's experience to expand beyond the walls of the school building in the course of the day. One successful example, an extensive environmental studies project, was so startling that it seems valuable to report it here.

This primary school is set in a modern housing development in Leicestershire. It is endowed with good teachers, a fine building and equipment, and has had good parental relations for some time. In the spring of 1969, the teacher of the oldest junior class (ten- and eleven-year-olds) thought of involving the children in writing their autobiographies. He felt this would bring the children into closer touch with their own family history and hoped it would also lead to a study involving the child, his parents, and the town. The study—"Me and My Community"—would incorporate reading, research, environmental work, and active participation in civic events.

With the support and assistance of the head teacher, the parents of the thirty-five children in the class came to a meeting to discuss plans. Part of the head's aim was to make sure they liked the idea of such a long-term study and that they would be willing to participate in many ways. In general, the parents were intrigued.

Work started on the autobiographies over the summer vacation. Most parents talked willingly with their children, and only a few pupils failed to get a good start on the work. When school reopened in the fall, many autobiographies were nearly completed. The class began to work on the community study. They drew maps of the town and wrote descriptions of the area. They marked those places on the map that were of particular interest to them.

The teacher noticed that this first set of places reflected the interests of the parents: shops, garages, homes, and pubs. With further urging, the teacher persuaded the children to talk about their own special hideouts and haunts. Of twelve favorite locations (the culvert under the motorway, the vacant lot, the hidden corner of a farmer's field), ten were not legally open to the children. Parents and teachers were amazed by this discovery and talked at length about how many of these sites would have been perfectly legal for them to visit as children. The housing development, although suburban, had deeply circumscribed the life of the children.

As knowledge of the children's interests expanded, the project itself took off in a number of directions. Some children, interested in draftsmanship, drew plans of their own houses. Others set out to build models of their houses to scale, using miniature bricks and realistic building materials. Rich historical work came from examinations of the lives of older generations in the families. Fine writing was evident in many cases—enough to fill quite a few cardboard boxes with descriptive pieces, stories, essays, and poems. Math did not suffer either, for many children used complex calculations in their work.

As this project progressed, parents and other relatives became positively involved in much of the work that took place in the classroom and outside. Through autobiographies, trips to their parents' places of work, and the inquiries into the community, children and parents came to know one another better. The parent found a new basis for communication with the child after seeing him at work and joining him in an activity. The child came to understand just what his father did all day and what his job or profession meant to him. None of the teachers engaged in this project would argue that it was faultless, but it provided an exceptional level of involvement for the children and an intriguing approach to education for ten- and eleven-year-olds. Both the children and their teacher wished that they had had another year to devote to the study.

On a later visit to this school we immediately noticed

the deep relationships that had evolved between the teacher and the children in this particular group. When we arrived, they had just returned two days before from a trip to Wales. They had stayed at a Methodist youth camp on the Welsh coast and had explored the countryside, seashore, and town. Each child kept a brief diary while he was there and did additional writing every day—perhaps a thumbnail sketch of something he had seen, a description of the mood induced by low clouds over the sea, or a piece about the patterns of stones on the beach. The youth center gave each pupil a knapsack for collecting things, and most children returned to school with a load of mementos.

When we visited their classroom, we found it full of seaweed, fish nets, drawings, poems, shells, rocks, animal life from the beach, and all sorts of sketches and notes. The room hummed with activity. A list of ideas on the board had sparked off other projects. We were immediately struck by two girls who were making a plaster of paris sculpture on a large table in the corner. They had collected long, thin strands of bamboo and some beautiful pieces of driftwood on the beach. Their sculpture was based on the shapes of the wood; the bamboo strips were arched and intertwined over a board that held a gnarled piece of driftwood. The girls were molding a round plaster of paris shape which seemed to float above the thin curves of wood. In fact, they had bent the bamboo to give the maximum amount of support to the sculpture. It had taken them the best part of two days to achieve a shape that was strong enough to support the plaster of paris. They were very nervous about the outcome.

Another group was working on silk screening. The patterns they had designed were based on the sea:

fish patterns swam through seaweed. The designs that emerged were the result of a group effort and were only in the early stages when we arrived. On another table, two boys were building a dam, out of miniature bricks. They had seen a site on the trip which struck them as being ideal for a dam. When they returned, they reconstructed the land shapes from papier-mâché, did some reading on dam construction and materials, and then started to build a scale model. They would eventually test its strength with water. Next to them, pupils were working on some pieces of creative writing started on the trip. Others were making plaster of paris molds of shells and rocks or doing shell collages. Another group was using the textures of bark found on the beach for some printing.

In the library, in another part of the school, two boys who had become intrigued with the mountains in Wales had embarked on a major project. They hoped to discover how mountains were formed, where the highest peaks were located, how to tell the age of hills, and what could grow on different mountainsides. They found that they had to read some books on geography and geology to answer many of their questions.

As we talked to these boys in the library, a commotion began at the other end of the hall. Disaster had struck the two girls and their sculpture. As they were preparing to sand down the plaster of paris, the entire shape exploded and fell apart, leaving them with a board covered with white crumbled dust. They were, however, determined to try again; to experiment with different ways of supporting the sculpture. "We can't give up now!" they said in unison.

All this activity was in its early stages. Many of the initial projects would lead naturally to writing, to work in history, and to other areas. The exciting aspect of this trip was its impact on the class and the teacher who accompanied them. The head of the school, who joined the trip, felt that both he and the teacher had come to understand many of the children far better than they ever could in the classroom. When they had been in Wales—whether horseback riding, walking on the beach, or exploring the village—the children and adults were relaxed and thoroughly themselves, one of the most important advantages of leaving the school with children. Any trip outside the building puts both children and teachers in a different light. In an extended visit such as this one, the teacher can make discoveries about the children which might never be made in a class setting, and establish new points of contact with the group.

In this Leicestershire class, the staff members came as close as any teacher could to knowing their children well. They began with an important, and successful, involvement of parents and came to see what the children's real needs and interests were. They built on this knowledge through the shared experience of an unexplored site in Wales, where they could see the children away from both home and school. The children responded with outstanding work and with many honest expressions of feelings and ideas.

This movement away from the classroom and out into the community is a subject of great interest to many teachers, both in England and America. Some educators in England describe the future school as a shell; one head said it should be a "nice place to come in out of the rain." The building would, in effect, act as a workshop where projects, initiated and developed outside the classroom, could be completed. The school would hold the necessary equipment; it would be a center for the whole community as well as for children and teachers.

English educators who look toward true community schools tend to think in terms of small groups of children. A few counties have realized that the village school has great possibilities for this kind of work—and in these areas the two-, three- and four-teacher schools will be preserved where it is economically feasible. While these schools can be limiting, they are also the most natural of community centers and can easily involve parents and villagers in a variety of projects. A few areas have also acted to combat the isolation of the rural school and have arranged for exchanges of children—a confined, city group will come to the country school for a week, while the rural children explore the nearby city or large town. Sometimes parents are included on these residential visits as helpers and participants.

Unfortunately, this type of experience is an exception, as is the example of the children who studied "Me and My Community." In many senses, English experiments with community schools or more traditional parental involvement have not achieved the level of success of some American communities. Yet, in both countries, an essential part of the child will remain a mystery to the teacher until parents are effectively drawn into the life of the school.

A more crucial issue occurs when a school works along lines that the parent does not comprehend. Many of the newer approaches to children are misunderstood, especially in areas accustomed to more traditional schooling. This is less a problem in the infant schools—where more informal methods have gradually gained recognition and approval—than in the junior schools, which are just beginning to develop and change. New techniques of teaching mathematics are completely foreign to some parents as are classrooms where eight-, nine-, and ten-year-olds move from one place to another, talking freely and working on different tasks at the same time. These parents are hostile to methods that seem strange to them. Where once their children spent long hours in preparation for the eleven-plus exam, they now attend schools that seem radical in comparison. The parents can only feel negative toward a change which is not thoroughly explained to them.

A junior school in Oxfordshire demonstrated a successful and intelligent approach to this problem. The school had recently acquired a new head teacher and a number of new staff members, who altered the building and began to work informally with the children. Many parents, accustomed to hearing their children speak of school in terms of hours of homework and the strictness—or laxity—of individual teachers, were shocked to discover that their children were suddenly moving from one teacher to another in the course of a day and doing "whatever they wanted" to the extent of working on a single project for days at a time. The parents began to worry, and many rumors spread about the new staff.

The head teacher, however, was prepared for this reaction and decided to explain his ideas to the parents by involving them in the same kinds of learning that their children engaged in every day. In a series of evening workshops, parents began to understand "new" mathematics, for example, by measuring, counting, weighing, making graphs, and thinking about different problems and finding solutions.

By participating in these sessions—which were similar to good in-service courses for teachers—the parents discovered how much students of any age can learn from one another through talking and sharing in all kinds of activities. As mothers and fathers sat on the floor to measure the length of the classroom or walked to the back of the room to ask a teacher a question, they could see that learning does not always take place in enforced silence and immobility. They realized that different members of the group approached problems in a variety of ways. Teachers and parents found concrete issues to discuss, and the school's ideas became real to many people. "Learning by doing" was no longer a slogan, but a real experience for a number of adults. In addition to these evening sessions, parents were encouraged to drop in on the school at any time; later in the year, the school opened its doors to the community and large numbers of townspeople, not all of them parents, turned out to see the work in progress.

This effort involved long working hours for a time on the part of the staff, but the results were rewarding. Parents became more interested in cooperation and less concerned with complaints; the children felt more relaxed because of a reduction in tensions between home and school. In addition, some teachers realized that their methods were not always infallible and that some criticisms were well-founded. Changes were made which grew from shared concerns about children.

This is an example of an attempt at communication which rarely takes place in England or America. No school—whether working traditionally or engaging in informal practices—can hope to justify its goals by closing its doors to the parents. A close look at educational aims is always as valuable for an excellent school as it is for a bad one. Moreover, if teachers want to change the ways in which children learn, they must be sure that the parents understand the reasons behind new approaches. The best way to gain support is to involve the parents in learning itself and to demonstrate, at the same time, the differences that occur among children. This means removing the school from politics; it means reducing apathy and encouraging a constant sharing of ideas from home to school and from the classroom to the community. In the end, teachers and parents should find that there is much to discover together as they strive to come closer to the children.

CHAPTER THIRTEEN

Change in Our Schools

JOY IS A WORD that is seldom used to describe the atmosphere in a school building, yet it is one that occurred to us on numerous occasions as we observed children in some English schools. We saw children and teachers enjoying their days together and feeling that school is a happy place. We were struck with the energy and zest that accompanied much of the activity in the best classrooms, and we often wondered how the children's new-found happiness and sense of worth affected their lives outside school. We gained an important answer to this question on a visit to an urban school, where changes within the classroom led to a gradual transformation of values, experiences, and attitudes within the surrounding community.

The school had many of the characteristics of an impoverished institution in industrialized countries. A number of children lived in poor conditions and had been brutalized by a school experience familiar to many city dwellers in America. The teaching there had been strictly formal, for control over the children seemed to be the school's most important goal. Many teachers, unable to contain their classes or coerce them into an acceptance of middle-class values, left in despair. The rate of staff turnover was such that it was not unusual for a child to have three teachers in the course of a school year.

When a new head teacher arrived two years ago, the school was near collapse. Children were constantly engaged in fights; some would disappear from school for weeks at a time. Police watched the building to protect teachers from the wrath of parents and others in the area. Chaos reigned in most rooms, and learning was out of the question. The new head found children who could not read, write, paint, or talk. Despite this disastrous beginning, she has since created a changed environment which has had a profound effect on the surrounding neighborhood.

The head gradually recruited a staff of her own choosing. Together they planned a setting where learning was centered on individuals. There was great emphasis on the development of relationships between children and adults and between the children themselves. The staff began to run an informal day and worked long hours after school to reorganize and develop the curriculum. Thanks to some governmental aid, many essential renovations were carried out inside the building.

When we first saw this school, it bore little resemblance to the head's description of what it had been like. Where once fist fights had been the daily norm, the children were now settled and happy. They were engaged in purposeful activity and were beginning to see that learning could be important to them. Some children were starting to talk to adults about their work and to realize that what they liked, did, or thought was of concern to others. Instead of frightened, defensive staff members, we found a team of teachers who were eager to help the children as individuals. They accepted them for what they were and tried to use the children's interests as the basis for the curriculum. They were anxious to provide an atmosphere of trust which would overcome the children's earlier feelings about school. While many areas still needed work and improvement, they were well on their way to success.

Perhaps the most dramatic change that occurred in this school took place among the parents. From the very beginning, the new head opened the school to the community and had frequent meetings to explain methods of teaching, reasons for tearing down walls in the building, and new attitudes toward learning exhibited by the teachers. She found that many parents were inarticulate at first; like the children, they had never had the chance to talk with anyone about education. As the year went by, she brought them in repeatedly to talk, to observe, to participate. Slowly, the parents found a voice and became genuinely involved. Many began to spend time in the school, and the head teacher discovered a few mothers who were quietly learning to read over their children's shoulders.

This school was remarkable because it had such a profound effect on so many people. The children were happy, and they carried their new-found enjoyment into their homes. Parents began to know their children. They saw them open up and gradually lose their earlier tendencies to fight whenever they could. The time they spent in school with their children made valuable contributions to family relationships and enabled everyone —parents, children, and teachers—to communicate more effectively about immediate concerns, problems, hopes, and interests.

This school was still a long way from perfection when

we saw it, and tremendous hard work was involved in giving these opportunities to the children. Yet the school has achieved what we have yet to see in many American schools: an atmosphere where people care for one another, where children and parents are supported and encouraged for what they are, not what they should be. What the teachers said to their children in effect was: We respect you, and your parents, for yourselves. We are not going to try to make you into something else or deny the value of your world. We do not call you disadvantaged or culturally deprived, implying that your life is lacking in some way. We are going to use your talents and involve you and your families wholeheartedly in the process of learning. We seek friendship, and we seek positive growth and development—for you and for ourselves.

These teachers understood the true meaning of the words "community school," and they fought to create one, despite the early hostilities, the old building, and a broken and bitter community. They are proving that it is possible to involve all children—not just the rich or gifted—in learning; that it is possible to change some community attitudes through parental involvement in education. In this school in particular, we became more convinced than ever that Americans can benefit from the study of English primary education.

In many ways, the neighborhood these children lived in was similar to some in American cities, and their behavior in school similar to that of American children. From what we could learn of their early childhood experiences, we surmised that they had not had as strict and formal an upbringing as some English children receive in more affluent homes. There was more action and noise in these urban classrooms than in suburban primary schools elsewhere in England. Some children reflected the violence of their community. Yet they were working hard and well in an informal setting similar to those found in other areas. Our conviction that work of this kind can be successful with the urban poor was substantiated in three other English city schools, and supported by friends who have observed similar work in early stages of development in the city of Liverpool.

Although we contend that some comparisons between English and American children are valid, we do not assume that the sum total of the work now taking place in the better English schools should be exported whole to the United States. In America, there is the critical problem of understanding what underlies the English successes before attempts are made to apply their attitudes and methods. It is also important to consider English failures as well as achievements, for both bear valuable lessons for American teachers. An informal classroom, run without a complete knowledge of its inner workings and philosophy, is a miserable experience for the children and their teacher.

One infant school that we visited, located in a middle-income area just outside a small English city, contained many examples of misinformed teaching. At first glance, the teachers seemed to be using the "right" techniques. The children were doing a variety of things. Some were playing with water, others were pasting materials together, and a substantial number were writing diligently. "We're running an integrated day," said a stern faced lady.

In reality, something very different was taking place. For one thing, these teachers did not understand the value of play for children. The activities kept the children occupied so the teacher could get on with the "basics." Because the teacher did not take an active interest in what the children were doing, their play lacked spontaneity. They had obviously been using the same materials for a long time without any direction. In one room, a large group of children were working on reading. Nine of them stood in line next to the teacher's desk, waiting for her to check their stories. They looked bored and lifeless and the very fact that they had to stand in line suggested a failure in the integrated day.

This teacher felt that if the children were provided with individual writing books, easels, water tubs, puzzles, and sand, the classroom would come to life. The same pattern was repeated throughout the school. Unfortunately, the teaching in this school affirmed Nora Goddard's words, written in 1969:

> Active learning is still in the process of being understood and developed. A possible danger is that the classroom can easily become stereotyped. The provision of basic materials . . . may become automatic so that teachers cease to think about them, add to them, or present them differently. Active learning is perhaps only achieved when the teacher is active with her children, seeing the possibilities of materials and recognizing growing points.[1]

These teachers failed to see a great deal that was going on around them. On our visit to the school, we were accompanied by a lecturer from a college of education, a woman who has devoted years to training teachers and trying to encourage their understanding of the development and needs of children. As we left the building, she shared our feeling of despair about the school.

The teachers in the school seemed unaware of their problems and unable to criticize their own work. Although honest self-appraisal is difficult, a remarkable number of good teachers in England are never completely satisfied with their teaching. Their classrooms are dynamic and stimulating because they can question themselves; they are able to stand back and analyze the learning that takes place. Many do not assume that what is successful with one group of children will produce fine results with the next, and their classrooms change character from year to year.

In some instances, the colleges of education are to blame for teachers' misunderstandings of educational goals and philosophies. Some colleges teach their students to use gimmicks and set methods without giving them an adequate understanding of the aims that lie behind them. Others treat the students as if they were still children, or pupils enrolled in secondary school. Another cause of poor education occurs when a formal school suddenly decides to opt for informality, but lacks the leadership to guide the staff in the difficult transition. This is a common problem, recognized by many in England. A London school provides an example.

A new head teacher had recently taken over and announced to her staff that they must make use of informal methods. The head herself did not know what she meant when she said this. She wanted her school to follow the lead of others which were successful, but she did not realize that each school had to become informal in its own way based upon the children's needs, the teachers' abilities, and the facilities at hand. One traditional teacher panicked when she was told to run an informal classroom with an integrated day. The head's only instructions were to let the children choose their own activities and to permit them to do things when they wanted. To the teacher this meant a removal of the methods which had formerly guided her work with children. When she took away the old structure, she had nothing with which to replace it, and the children ran circles around her.

The plight of this teacher is typical of situations

caused by progressive education in the United States during the 1920's and 1930's. Traditional schools which felt they wanted to become progressive thought they could do so only if they allowed the children absolute freedom. John Dewey was very much concerned with this problem, stating:

> . . . the traditional school . . . was not a group or community held together by participation in common activities. Consequently, the normal, proper conditions for control were lacking. Their absence was made up for, and to a considerable extent had to be made up for, by the direct intervention of the teacher, who, as the saying went, "KEPT order." He kept it because order was in the teacher's keeping, instead of residing in the shared work being done.[2]

When this order is removed, no matter where the school may be, both children and teachers need help in finding a new basis for interaction. Support from the head teacher or principal is vital. The success of informal classes often depends upon his judgment and leadership. Not every teacher need drop traditional practices in the same way or at the same time. Dorothy Gardner, commenting on infant schools, has noted: "Every fresh development in . . . education seems to require additions to the equipment of a good teacher, but never the discarding of the qualities that made a really good teacher of the older methods."[3]

Years before, in the United States, Dewey had lamented the foundation of many progressive schools which had been established in a negative response to formal education:

> The problems are not even recognized, to say nothing of being solved, when it is assumed that it suffices to reject the ideas and practices of the old education and then go to the opposite extreme . . . [M]any of the newer schools tend to make little or nothing of organized subject-matter of study; to proceed as

if any form of direction and guidance by adults were an invasion of individual freedom, and as if the idea that education
should be concerned with the present and future meant that
acquaintance with the past has little or no role to play in education.[4]

English primary school staffs are not generally adopt-
ing informal methods with the thought that the children in their charge need a totally free environment or
that the school must abandon all previous practices.
Yet it is perfectly possible that American teachers
might think about informal methods as a complete
break from the past, just as some had approached progressive education in the 1920's and 1930's.

For many reasons, progressive education never
reached any large segment of the public schools in
America. If the informal methods now advocated by
some people in the United States are to have any
greater influence, they must be implemented with careful thought and critical judgment.

Substantial misinformation already exists in the
United States about modern practices in English primary schools. We have heard it said that what is going
on in England is simply an extension of the old American progressive education movement; that it has been
tried before and failed. We hope that the descriptions
in this book will help to negate this belief. Some reports
have indicated that informal methods are being practiced in most schools throughout England—a revela-
tion to active educators in England who are working
hard to gain support for new approaches in many areas
where change has been unknown for years. Another
false idea is that these methods originated with the
Leicestershire Plan. Leicestershire has never laid claim
to a master plan for primary schools, although the
county's excellent advisory service works hard to pro-

mote a variety of thoughtful changes in classrooms and whole schools.

Perhaps the worst misinformation heard in the United States is that English primary schools practice unstructured freedom, for which we may read "chaos." Although unruliness has occurred in some few classrooms, it is far from the norm. These English primary schools do not represent the philosophies of "free schools" that have developed in the United States. Nor do they reflect large-scale acceptance of the views of A. S. Neill, the Englishman whose book, *Summerhill,* has received wide attention. Rather, the good classes remain well-structured—in their own ways—with the teacher making a number of conscious decisions about who should do what and when it should be done. Extensive planning and the keeping of careful records are vital to these classrooms and teachers usually devote more time to these activities than they would in a traditional classroom.

Americans may have developed some of their inaccurate ideas through school visits which have been both cursory and nonrepresentative. As part of a steady stream of visitors to England, we became worried by the large number of Americans who come for a ten-day visit, see six or eight exciting schools, and return to the United States ready to "work in the English way." Such surface experiences tend to produce the belief that techniques can be standardized and that the revolution in English primary schools has occurred throughout the country.

A more serious problem, however, is the one now faced by English educators of what to do with all the Americans who come to see their schools. The good schools have been so saturated with visitors that they often face grave disruptions. As visitors who have been part of this influx, we hope that Americans will develop and observe their own models and allow the English schools to catch their breath. A growing number of teachers in the United States are giving children a more exciting and individual education, and it is to these teachers and children that we should begin to turn for help and inspiration.

The English experience demonstrates that the somewhat half-hearted reforms that we have begun in America will never really modify the quality of the education our children receive. For example, the widely known E.S.S. science program offers some fine opportunities for American children and teachers. Pupils can make discoveries and engage in exciting projects, but unless the attitudes toward learning that underpin the program permeate the rest of the curriculum, the few hours spent on science each week will do little for a child's development. Similarly, some of the fine reading programs available to American teachers, encouraging broad approaches to learning to read, will make negligible accomplishments if the classroom is not flexible, or if, for instance, reading is followed by math that is presented in a strict, formal manner, with no relation between these subjects in the teacher's mind.

In fields other than curriculum reform, American efforts again do not have the breadth of English accomplishments. Individualized instruction, as it is so often called, is a prime example. This form of instruction is based on the idea that a child can be taught individually —usually subject by subject. But in workshops and education courses that deal with individualized instruction, the issue of whether present curricula are suited to this method of learning is seldom discussed. Individualized instruction still assumes that the teacher does all the instruction with little change in content, which is contrary to much educational thought in England at the present. The aim of good teachers in England is not to encourage new systems of education, but rather new philosophical attitudes toward learning.

The switch to a wholly different setting for children requires a great intellectual jump on the part of the teacher. He must abandon the idea of a teacher-directed classroom and develop attitudes which consider many facets of individual learning in which the child's needs and aims play an important part. A few American teachers have made this transition, but apparently not as many as in England. Teachers in England have not accomplished this work in isolation, and some factors which have helped them could become essential aspects of work in American schools.

The first substantial aid to the English teacher is the independence of his school. In the United States, greater freedom of choice for individual schools, akin to the situation in England, could encourage a more thoughtful approach to children and education. The teacher should not be bound by stringent curriculum guides or by the feeling that some superior intellect must prepare the subject matter for him to teach. A teaching staff with discretion in these matters can engage in productive debate about the relative value of their methods and subjects. Different schools can find a variety of ways to work with the children. To achieve this situation, the teacher needs strong support. He needs to feel that his ideas are important. Just as the child sees that he plays an essential role in his own learning, so the teacher should feel that he can make a contribution to innovation in education. These English schools have shown that teachers who can participate in this way are often better teachers because of it.

The advisory systems in some areas of England offer the crucial support required by the teacher. There is nothing comparable to advisory services in American school systems. Some are too small to effectively support such a service, but many could do so if they were willing to finance a nonadministrative group with loosely defined tasks. Outside of the school systems themselves, only the action centers, funded by Title Three of the 1965 Education Act, offer any possibility of becoming real advisory services. Yet their finances are failing and their relations with the school systems are sometimes far from cordial. Experience in England, however, indicates that the communication the advisory services could provide would be vital to promoting change in American elementary schools.

Another difficulty with American schools is that so many are so large. English schools are able to deal with learning in an imaginative way when they work with a relatively small number of children, even though individual classes are far too big. Neither an adviser nor anyone else can accomplish much in a school of eight hundred children in which the head teacher knows only a few students well and is sometimes unaware of his staff's concerns. A school of two or three hundred children—or less—permits outside help to be more successful and allows for greater communication. A smaller school creates a setting which is not only more personal but more comprehensible and enjoyable for the children.

Independence, advisory services, and small schools could all contribute to the success of American education. In addition, there are two other factors which we should consider, the first concerning our priorities.

Even though English primary schools often lack sufficient funds, and despite the difficult period through which the English economy has passed, the central government has made clear its interest in education. It recognizes the importance of its human resources and is now spending more on education than on defense. In the United States, we seem a long way from such an orientation of priorities. This is not to argue that all American schools need more funds. They do, however, need to recognize that major changes of a basic nature are required.

Second, we could benefit from new attitudes of tolerance in our evaluation of programs. The changes in English schools have taken years to develop. No one in England would apply a form of instant evaluation to a new educational idea. Yet an English head teacher on a trip to the United States was shocked to meet principals who felt a program must prove its worth in a measurable fashion in six to nine months. This approach is detrimental to change of any kind. We must be prepared to wait for proof of success and we must give teachers and children time to find new ways of working together. If we allowed teachers to work in a school for five years or more, developing learning which is grounded in the interests of the children, we could demonstrate successes that could never be achieved in nine months.

We hope that Americans who are interested in educational change will go beyond our descriptions of English classrooms and look closely at other material on the subject. We have attempted to present a view of some exceptional schools, although their methods and attitudes toward children are still in the minority in England. For every good school we have described, there are others where practices are probably archaic, where learning is teacher-directed, the head teacher autocratic, and the teachers unaware of new ways of looking at children. Other British and American writers are sensitive to both the strengths and weaknesses of the English system, and their views are worth serious consideration.

A very critical evaluation of English primary education could—and should—be written. British educators in particular need to continue to look closely at their own system, realizing its merits while proposing constructive criticism and advice. One area warranting appraisal is the deeply entrenched class system and its effects on the children. Even in the best schools, some teachers assume that middle-class values are the only ones worthy of emulation. When this feeling is conveyed to children in slum-area schools, especially those in immigrant neighborhoods, a patronizing attitude often appears. We were astounded to encounter one head teacher who put her arm around a pretty West Indian girl and said to us, "Isn't it *amazing* how well she does in school? We never would have dreamed she could do so well—considering her background." This woman was entirely oblivious to the feelings of the confused child beside her—nor did she notice the embarrassment this remark caused us. Statements of this nature, often made within hearing distance of the child, are not uncommon. They raise serious questions about the future of race relations in England as well as the sensitivity of some teachers to the needs and capabilities of their children.

The British also need to pursue more long-term studies of informal classes, following the child from the last stage of junior school up through secondary school. We need to know whether a formal and sometimes grim secondary school negates the child's former experiences at the primary level. Evaluation of this kind could build on the studies already undertaken, which have pointed to the short-term successes of good informal classrooms. There is no doubt that the children in the best schools are happy, that they find school enjoyable, and that the standard of their work is extremely high. What effect do these same schools have on their later life?

With careful thought, aspects of work in English primary schools can be applied to schools in the United States. Yet it bears repeating that what is taking place in England is not a system or program that is easily imported. Its basis is an attitude which deals with children as individuals who have a right to enjoy learning and to be themselves. In order to teach in this fashion, the teacher must look beyond new projects and curriculum ideas to the basic needs and interests of each child. He must find ways in which to mesh the children's interests with his own to promote forms of learning important to them all.

Notes

INTRODUCTION

[1] "Leicestershire Plan" accurately applies to the innovative system of secondary education which has developed in that county.

[2] G. W. Basset, *Innovation in Primary Education* (London, Wiley Interscience, 1970), p. 16.

[3] Central Advisory Council for Education (England), *Children and Their Primary Schools*, Vol. 1 (London, Her Majesty's Stationery Office, 1967), para. 270. Referred to throughout this book as the Plowden Report.

[4] The term "infant" may be misleading, since it is now generally applied to very young children. We use it here because it is still the common term for English schools working with five- to seven-year-olds. Infant schools and junior schools (for seven- to eleven-year-olds) are sometimes united as two departments of one primary school.

[5] Local education authorities (L.E.A.) are the county or city councils that oversee the schools in their area. There are 148 such authorities of many different sizes in England.

CHAPTER ONE

[1] "Hall" is used throughout this book in the English sense of a large multipurpose room used for dining, physical education, assemblies, and special displays.

[2] Educational Priority Areas were established by the British government in July, 1967. They are distinct urban and rural areas in which the schools get substantial financial and other aid to counteract social deprivation. With the cooperation of universities, extensive research is going on in five areas, concerning local problems and the work of the projects themselves.

[3] This class involves some unusual uses of apparatus and may include some dance or movement. It is discussed further in Chapter Nine.

CHAPTER TWO

[1] George Dennison, *The Lives of Children* (New York, Random House, 1969), p. 212.

[2] There are two booklets which provide an outline of the series and discuss implications of teaching Nuffield Math. They are Nuffield Mathematics Project, *I Do and I Understand* (London, Chambers-Murray, 1967) and *The Story So Far* (London, Chambers-Murray, 1969).

[3] Lesley Webb, *Modern Practice in the Infant School* (Oxford, Basil Blackwell, 1969), pp. 30–31.

[4] Some schools in England employ the initial teaching alphabet, or i.t.a., to aid in the first steps of learning to read. There is a substantial body of literature and research data supporting i.t.a.; however, among teachers with whom we talked, we found remarkable discouragement and disinterest. Complaints centered on the limits of i.t.a. in that it must be used with all the children in the class. Some teachers of eight- and nine-year-olds reported that they saw little difference in the reading abilities of children who had used i.t.a. and those who had not.

[5] Cuisenaire rods are blocks of different lengths, each having a specific color. Values may be assigned to the blocks, which a child can use to aid in many forms of counting. Dienes blocks include unit cubes, ten-rods, hundred-squares, and thousand-cubes as well as blocks to allow counting in bases three, four, five, and six.

CHAPTER THREE

[1] Mary A. Mycock, "Vertical Grouping," in Vincent R. Rogers, ed. *Teaching in the British Primary School* (New York, The MacMillan Company, 1970), p. 58.

[2] Three government reports under the chairmanship of Sir Henry Hadow: *The Education of the Adolescent* (London, H.M.S.O.,

1926); *The Primary School* (London, H.M.S.O., 1931); *Infant and Nursery Schools* (London, H.M.S.O., 1933). The reports related to primary education are discussed in Chapter Seven.

³ Joan C. B. Lunn, *Streaming in the Primary School* (Slough, Buckinghamshire, National Foundation for Educational Research, 1970).

⁴ Colleges of education provide the three-year training course which is necessary for qualification as a teacher. Some now offer a fourth year, ending in the award of a degree known as the Bachelor of Education (B. Ed.).

⁵ Plowden Report, paragraphs 361–363.

CHAPTER FOUR

¹ Charity James, *Young Lives at Stake* (London, Collins, 1968), p. 19.

² *Ibid.*, p. 107.

³ Elementary Science Study, or E.S.S., was founded in 1959 and is now a part of the Educational Development Center, Newton, Massachusetts.

⁴ Leonard Marsh, *Alongside the Child in the Primary School* (London, A. & C. Black, 1970), p. 82.

⁵ Marsh, *Let's Explore Mathematics* (London, A. & C. Black).

CHAPTER FIVE

¹ John Dewey, *Experience and Education* (London, Collier-Macmillan), p. 62.

CHAPTER SIX

¹ London *Times*, "Educational Supplement," February 20, 1970.

² Except in the cases of denominational schools, these boards are made up mainly of members appointed by the local authority.

³ This is discussed more fully in Chapter Ten.

⁴ Rhodes Boyson, "Who Teaches the Teachers?" *New Statesman*, May 9, 1970.

⁵ London *Times*, "Educational Supplement," February 13, 1970.

⁶ Marsh, *Alongside the Child in the Primary School* (London, A. & C. Black, 1970), p. 114.

CHAPTER SEVEN

[1] G. W. Bassett, *Innovation in Primary Education,* (London, Wiley Interscience, 1970), p. 126.
[2] Her Majesty's Inspectorate of Schools, or H.M.I. Their role is discussed later in this chapter.
[3] In 1967, the Plowden Report (para. 947) estimated that about 50 authorities, out of 162, maintained an advisory service of some kind. Many more authorities could benefit from the service.
[4] Plowden Report, para. 1013.
[5] Ibid, para. 1020.
[6] Geoffrey Caston, "Schools Council Defended," in the London *Times,* "Educational Supplement," April 10, 1970.
[7] From the *Tabulated Reports on Schools Inspected in Oxford, Berkshire, Northamptonshire* and *Leicester,* 1858-9.
[8] John Blackie, *Inside the Primary School* (London, Her Majesty's Stationery Office, 1967), pp. 136-137.
[9] G. W. Bassett, *op. cit.,* p. 3.

CHAPTER EIGHT

[1] P. Woodham-Smith in Evelyn Lawrence, ed., *Friedrich Froebel and English Education* (London, University of London Press, 1952), p. 22.
[2] Plowden Report, vol. I, para. 510.
[3] Willem van der Eyken and Barry Turner, *Adventures in Education* (London, Allen Lane, The Penguin Press, 1969).
[4] We are indebted to Dorothy Gardner for her thoughts on the role that Susan Isaacs played in English education. Miss Gardner has recently completed *Susan Isaacs, The First Biography* (London, Methuen, 1969). For a further discussion of developments in primary schools during the past forty years, see also D.E.M. Gardner and Joan E. Cass, *The Role of The Teacher in the Infant and Nursery School* (Oxford, Pergamon, 1965).
[5] Nuffield Mathematics Project, "General Introduction," appearing in all the booklets.

CHAPTER NINE

[1] Blackie, *loc. cit.,* pp. 125-26.
[2] Rudolph Laban, *Modern Educational Dance* (London, MacDonald and Evans, 1948), p. 7

[3] *Ibid.,* p. 95

[4] Diana Jordan, *Childhood and Movement* (Oxford, Basil Blackwell, 1966), p. 3

[5] Laban, *op. cit.,* p. 30

[6] *Ibid.,* pp. 22–23.

[7] Jordan, *op. cit.,* p. 74

[8] *Ibid.,* p. 3

[9] Molly Brearley, ed., *First Years in School* (London, George Harrap, 1967), p. 212.

[10] Laban, *op. cit.,* p. 93.

[11] Laban, *The Mastery of Movement* (London, MacDonald and Evans, 1960), p. 17.

CHAPTER TEN

[1] John Holt, "To the Rescue," in *New York Review of Books,* October 9, 1969, p. 30.

[2] Figure taken from Plowden Report, Vol. I, para. 1081, table 29 and adjusted.

[3] Plowden Report, Vol. I, para. 1087.

[4] Ibid, para. 1092.

[5] Ibid, para. 1093.

[6] Ibid, para. 1094.

CHAPTER ELEVEN

[1] *Nuffield Junior Science Teacher's Guides; Apparatus; Animals and Plants,* four vol., (London, Collins, 1967).

[2] *Science 5/13* (London, MacDonald, 1969).

[3] Reported by Linda Christmas, "Breakout to Green Fields", *Times Educational Supplement,* April 3, 1970, pp. 18–19.

CHAPTER TWELVE

[1] Plowden Report, para. 127.

CHAPTER THIRTEEN

[1] Nora L. Goddard, *Reading in the Modern Infants' School* (London, University of London Press, 1969), p. 9.

[2] John Dewey, *Experience and Education* (New York, Collier, 1963), p. 55.

[3] Dorothy E. M. Gardner and Joan E. Cass, *The Role of the Teacher in the Infant and Nursery School* (Oxford, Pergamon, 1965), p. 2.

[4] Dewey, *Experience and Education,* p. 22.

Schools Visited

In presenting this list of schools, we do not intend to single out any one group. Included here are some outstanding schools, schools with substantial reputations, and others which are far from satisfactory. To the children, teachers, and head teachers of them all, we owe our thanks for the opportunity to visit, invade their classrooms, and talk about the work in progress and their plans for the future.

SCHOOL	HEAD TEACHER
OXFORDSHIRE	
Brookside Primary School, Bicester	Mr. Sidney Ing
Eynsham Primary School, Eynsham	Mr. George Baines
Finmere Primary School, Finmere	Miss Olive Bates
Goring Primary School, Goring-on-Thames	Mr. D. Williams
Great Haseley Primary School, Great Haseley	Mr. Walker
Hill View Primary School, Banbury	Mr. G. W. Eccles
John Hampden Junior School, Thame	Mr. Vernon Hale
Kidlington Infants' School, Kidlington	Miss Olive Keddie

Milton-Under-Wychwood Primary
   School, Milton-Under-Wychwood   Mr. Tom Brennan
Speedwell Infants' School, Littlemore   Miss M. Medhurst
Tower Hill Primary School, Witney   Mr. Tom John

LONDON (Inner London Education Authority)
Allen Edwards Infants' School   Mrs. C. E. Woolston
Bevington Infants' School   Mrs. Glen Fair
Bevington Junior School   Mr. K. Booker
Bousfield Infants' School   Mrs. M. G. McKenzie
Brunswick Park Infants' School   Miss Wendla Kernig
George Eliot Junior School   Miss M. M. Gray
Paddington Green Primary School   Mr. R. Perkin
Pooles Park Infants' School   Mrs. M. A. Clarke
Vittoria Primary School   Miss R. Shaw
Chelsea Open Air Nursery (Private)   Miss M. Marchant

LEICESTERSHIRE
Belton Primary School, Belton   Mrs. P. D. Saddington
Fernvale Primary School, Thurnby   Mr. K. C. Osborne
Ravenhurst Junior School, Braunstone   Mr. W. G. Hazel
Sherrard Infants' School, Melton
   Mowbray   Mrs. Mary Brown
Stafford Leys Primary School, Leicester
   Forest East   Mr. Gordon Hill

BRISTOL
Baptist Mills Infants' School   Mrs. E. Griese
Barton Hill Nursery and Infants' School   Mrs. B. Tutaev
Henbury Court Infants' School   Miss M. Kaye
Sea Mills Infants' School   Miss D. Nash

THE WEST RIDING OF YORKSHIRE
Archbishop of York's School,
   Bishopthorpe   Mr. Alan Clementson
Swallownest Primary School, Sheffield   Mr. R. Smith
Woodlesford Primary School,
   Woodlesford   Mr. D. Darton

EAST SUFFOLK AND IPSWICH
Clifford Road Primary School, Ipswich   Mr. Archie Llewellyn
Downing Primary School, Ipswich   Mr. D. Duncan
Kesgrave Infants' School, Kesgrave   Miss Jewell

Belstead Annex, Keswick Hall College of Education, Ipswich.
Froebel Institute, College of Education, Roehampton, London.
The Lady Spencer Churchill College of Education, Wheatley, Oxfordshire.
St. John's College of Education, York.

Acknowledgments

One of the most rewarding aspects of the year we spent in England was the warm and extensive cooperation which greeted us all over the country at every level of education. Our greatest debt of thanks goes to those teachers and children who permitted us to observe them at work, occupy their free time with questions and conversation, and return repeatedly throughout the year. These men, women, and children, who are not named here, were remarkably kind and open to all sorts of comments and disruptions and were generous with their thoughts about learning and teaching.

Of great help in initiating this project, encouraging it, and reading the manuscript were Jay Featherstone and Maurice Kogan — wise and kind people.

Throughout the year, individuals who work in many fields of education were generous with their time, thoughts, and friendship. Among these were Dorothy Gardner, John Blackie, Molly Brearley, Geoffrey and Sonya Caston, and Anne Corbett.

We are grateful to a number of people who work directly with education authorities and made important contributions to the project: John Coe and Katherine Jenkins in Oxfordshire; Tony Kallet, William Browse, and John and Dorothy Paull in Leicestershire; Andrew Sparkes in Bristol; Sir Alec Clegg in the West Riding of Yorkshire; and Nora Goddard in London.

Among many fine head teachers, we owe particular thanks to Tom Brennan, Mrs. E. Griese, Vernon Hale, Gordon Hill, Sidney Ing, Miss D. Nash, and Mrs. Peggy Saddington.

In the field of teacher education, Bob Smith, James Fairbairn, Mrs. Joan Tamburrini, Miss J. E. Johnson, Pauline Gilmore, and F. M. White contributed to our understanding of some fine teacher education projects and their relation to work in classrooms.

Elsewhere, we gained from talking with Geoffrey McCabe about museum services and with Eileen Molony about films. We are also grateful to Colin Nichols and to Mac McDonald for the time they spent explaining special projects in their classrooms.

Particular thanks are due to Strobe Talbot, Neil Jorgensen, Helen Featherstone, and Dick and Barbara Ketchum for reading some or all of various drafts and giving valued counsel.

While all those mentioned above made invaluable contributions to our project, any final errors naturally remain our responsibility.

A generous travel grant from Editorial Projects for Education in Washington, D.C., made possible our extensive visits to schools throughout England during the year. To them and to American Heritage Press go thanks for supporting our work throughout.

Bibliography

We have divided this section into three units. The first deals with books of some research value. The second mentions general descriptive books useful to teachers and others concerned with primary schools. The third unit notes useful books in particular areas of the curriculum, especially mathematics, science, and movement.

In the field of research

The most recent substantial research effort on English primary education, and perhaps the most valuable, is the Plowden Report, prepared by the Central Advisory Council for Education (England) and titled *Children and their Primary Schools,* Volume 1, *Report;* Volume 2, *Research and Surveys* (London, Her Majesty's Stationery Office, 1967). The previous government report on primary schools, also important in its time, is *Report of the Consultative Committee on the Primary School* (London, H.M.S.O., 1931) known as the Hadow Report.

Plowden generated substantial comment. Pieces related to it and of value today are: *Juniors—A Postscript to Plowden,* by Arthur Razzell (Harmondsworth, Penguin, 1968); Peters (ed.), *Perspectives on Plowden* (London, Routledge, Kegan, Paul, 1969); and the sometimes caustic *Black Paper Two,* edited by C. B. Cox and A. E. Dyson (London, Critical Quarterly Society, 1969).

No single work offers adequate historical perspective on change in primary schools. Some may be gained, however, from three books: Evelyn Lawrence, *Friedrich Froebel and English Education* (London, University of London Press, 1952); Dorothy Gardner's adulatory *Susan Isaacs: the First Biography* (London, Methuen Educational Ltd, 1969); and Willem van der Eyken and Barry Turner, *Adventures in Education* (London, Allen Lane the Penguin Press, 1969). The latter offers some intriguing sketches of a few schools and individuals, notably Susan Isaacs and the Malting House School. Chapters on the history of primary education over the last seventy years appear in a number of more general books, cited below.

In the realm of research directed specifically at English primary-age children and their schools, there are a number of other interesting books. In the *Role of the Teacher in Infant and Nursery School* (Oxford, Pergamon, 1965), Dorothy Gardner and Joan E. Cass discuss changes in teachers' roles in informal classrooms. Miss Gardner presents convincing evidence that informal classes are superior to more traditional ones in *Experiment and Tradition in the Primary Schools* (London, Methuen, 1966). Stan Gooch, Pringle, and Kellmer present evidence in a similar, but more recent, four-year study in *Four Years On* (London, Longmans Green, 1966), although their conclusions are less dramatic and their techniques somewhat confusing. Joan C. Barker Lunn presents a graphic case against ability-grouped classes in *Streaming in the Primary School* (Slough, Bucks, National Foundation for Educational Research in England and Wales, 1970).

In another area of research, Iona and Peter Opie delve in depth into games children play inside and outside of school in England. Their book, *Children's Games in Street and Playground* (Oxford, Clarendon Press, 1969), chronicles many games and contains valuable comments on the ways in which children make rules.

In a recently published book, Anna Freud reveals data collected over many years and continues her contribution toward an understanding of childhood. *Research at the Hampstead Child-Therapy Clinic* (London, Hogarth, 1970) has applications far beyond English schools and children. In another vein, but also with wide applications, is G. W. Bassett's *Innovations in Primary Education* (London, Wiley, 1970). The author's categories of English innovations, contrasted to those in the United States, are both revealing and depressing.

In many conversations about English primary schools and their work, Jean Piaget's name is heard. Translations of his works have been steadily published by Routledge, Kegan, Paul in London. The most important to many English educators seem to be

The Language and Thought of the Child, The Child's Conception of Number, The Origins of Intelligence in Children, and *The Moral Development of the Child.* Few teachers, however, have grappled with Piaget's prose and their knowledge of his work comes largely from articles and explanatory chapters in other books. In the same framework as Piaget's efforts lies Susan Isaacs' *Intellectual Growth in Young Children* (London, Routledge, Kegan, Paul, 1930), a book which is still widely read in England.

Among attempts to evolve a philosophy of modern primary education, R. F. Dearden's work stands as the most substantial recent piece. In *The Philosophy of Primary Education* he makes cogent points about informal methods of teaching, but leads the reader over some very confusing logic.

In thinking about American schools during a year of work in England, we found four books of particular help: John Dewey's *Experience and Education* (New York, Macmillan, 1938) and Lawrence A. Cremin's *The Transformation of the School* (New York, Knopf, 1968) deal with the same difficult but intriguing period in the history of education. Philip W. Jackson reveals some surprising and upsetting figures about contacts between children and teachers in *Life in Classrooms* (New York, Holt, Rinehart, and Winston, 1968). George Dennison, on the other hand, suggests some possibilities of what schools might be like in *The Lives of Children* (New York, Random House, 1969).

DESCRIPTIVE BOOKS OF USE TO TEACHERS AND OTHERS

It may be useful to present this category of books in order of the age groups they deal with. A good report on the preschool work going on in England and some of the problems the country must face in that area is Willem van der Eyken's *The Pre-School Years* (Harmondsworth, Penguin, 1969). But this area is not as well represented in literature as the infant school, on which there are a number of helpful books.

In two books, Molly Brearley has presented substantial information and advice for those working with infant-school children. *First Years in School* (London, G. Harrap for University of London Institute of Education, 1967), which she edited, has received wider acclaim than the committee-written *Fundamentals in the First School* (Oxford, Basil Blackwell, 1969). Both, however, are helpful and reflect to some extent the work going on at the Froebel Institute College of Education, where Miss Brearley was principal.

Also of use in work with the five- to seven-year-olds is Lesley Webb's *Modern Practice in the Infant School* (Oxford, Basil Blackwell, 1969). Webb offers concise suggestions about room arrangements, materials, and so on.

Dealing with the entire range of primary education, but with emphasis on junior schools, is Leonard Marsh's *Alongside the Child in the Primary School* (London, A. & C. Black, 1970). This is an insightful book by a man who has worked in primary schools in many capacities. One subject which he discusses is the many faceted integrated day. Interested readers should also turn to *The Integrated Day in the Primary School* (London, Ward Lock, 1968), by Mary Brown and Norman Precious, for further information on this important subject.

Two edited compilations provide the points of view of many fine teachers on a variety of subjects related to primary schools. Stewart Mason, the Director of Education in Leicestershire, carefully assembled *In Our Experience: the Changing Schools of Leicestershire* (London, Longman, 1970). Specifically for American readers, Vincent Rogers edited *Teaching in the British Primary School* (New York, Macmillan, 1970), a readily accessible and helpful book.

Also easy for Americans to locate are Joseph Featherstone's series of articles in *The New Republic*. Reprinted as a pamphlet, the first three articles are titled "The Primary School Revolution in Britain." They appeared in August and September, 1967. In a few pages, Featherstone reports on the successes of some schools in England and puts forward cogent arguments in favor of informal classrooms.

Americans may also look forward to a series of fine pamphlets on primary education, written in England and sponsored by the Schools Council and the Ford Foundation. They should be published in late 1971.

Of the wide range of descriptive and analytic books available today, none offers a better, over-all picture of British primary education than John Blackie's *Inside the Primary School* (London, H.M.S.O., 1967). Although the book was written largely for parents in England and other citizens who wondered what was happening in the primary schools, it is a fine introduction to the pros and cons of informal education for anyone concerned.

For a glimpse of work in progress in English secondary schools, Robin Pedley's *The Comprehensive School* (Harmondsworth, Penguin, 1963) is helpful. On another level, and considering both primary and secondary education in England, is Charity James's sensitive *Young Lives at Stake* (Glasgow, Collins, 1968) in which she proposes some massive changes in secondary work that would bring it more in line with children's experiences in informal primary schools.

In mathematics, three recent books survey work in progress and make concrete suggestions about curriculum in the schools. Of particular note is the Association of Teachers of Mathematics' *Notes of Mathematics in Primary Schools* (Cambridge, Cambridge University Press, 1968). Famous and valuable is the Schools Council's *Mathematics in the Primary School, Curriculum Bulletin No. 1,* third edition (London, H.M.S.O., 1969). Most recent is *Primary Mathematics, a Further Report* (London, 1970) by the Mathematical Association. This helpful book surveys the changes in math since the Association brought out its provocative report in 1955.

Perhaps of more immediate use in the classroom is the series published by the Nuffield Mathematics Project (London, W. & R. Chambers and John Murray, 1967). In nearly twenty pamphlets the Project deals with a wide range of mathematical work, approaches to new subject matter, and methods of checking on children's successes. The pamphlets are not uniformly excellent, but they surpass everything else available at the moment.

Also of use is Leonard Marsh's four-volume *Let's Explore Mathematics* (London, A. & C. Black, 1964; New York, Arco Publishing, 1966), although it is very easy to let them become mere workbooks in the classroom which is not what the author intended. For work in different bases, the teacher's guide for Z. P. Dienes' *Multi-Base Arithmetic Blocks* (Educational Supply Association, Harlow, Essex) is useful, as are the expensive blocks themselves.

In science work, *Nuffield Junior Science* (London, Collins, 1967) still stands as the finest guide available. Published by the Nuffield Foundation, the main series consists of four volumes: *Teacher's Guide 1 & 2, Animals and Plants,* and *Apparatus.* The ideas in the books, however, have proved very difficult to teach, and some of the authors (Bainbridge, Stockdale, and Wastnedge) have joined together to produce the valuable *Junior Science Source Book* (London, Collins, 1969).

Much advice about reading is contained in the more general books mentioned above, and further help comes from Nora Goddard's *Reading in the Modern Infant School* (London, University of London Press, 1969, revised edition).

In the realm of physical education and movement, Rudolph Laban's books are some of the classics: his *Modern Educational Dance* (London, McDonald and Evans, 1948) is very hard to find in the United States, but more accessible is the reprint of *The Mastery of Movement* (London, McDonald and Evans, 1960). Diana Jordan's *Childhood and Movement* (Oxford, Basil Blackwell, 1966) follows Laban's work carefully, applying it well to primary-school work.

The Inner London Education Authority's *Movement Education for Infants* offers excellent proposals for running both creative movement and physical education classes. The Department of Education and Science also provides good suggestions and fine photographs in the two-volume series *Physical Education in the Primary School,* part 1, *Moving and Growing* (London, H.M.S.O., 1952), and part 2, *Planning the Programme* (1953). J. M. Tanner emphasizes the importance of physical development vis-à-vis intellectual development in *Educational and Physical Growth* (London, University of London Press, 1961).

In crafts, the best single source of materials and information is the Dryad Press, which publishes a fine series of leaflets (Leicester, England, and Woodridge, N.J.).

Tying all of this work together into a marvelous world of education for children is Elwyn Richardson in his joyful *In the Early World* (New York, Pantheon, 1964). Although Richardson is a New Zealander and has made no great study of English primary schools, this beautifully illustrated chronicle of his work with children suggests what can happen anywhere in an informal classroom with intelligent thought and direction.

Some of the books published in England and mentioned here can be found in major bookstores in the United States. It is generally wisest, however, to order books directly from an English bookseller. This also lessens the cost of the book for an American purchaser.

A good bookseller to contact in England is Blackwell's, Broad Street, Oxford, England. They will advise you of the cost of the book, if you wish, or they will send the book and bill you at the same time. It is also possible to open an account with them in U.S. dollars. Books sent by sea arrive in six to eight weeks. For faster delivery, they can be sent by air at substantially greater cost.